ANCHORED
by GRACE

HOW ONE MAN'S FAITH
TRANSFORMED LOSS INTO MIRACLES

KEITH ISBELL

CONTENTS

My brother, S. Kyle Isbell, brought the idea of writing a book together early in 2012. He said, "it could be a bright story in an otherwise dark time for others". Kyle died on July 1, 2012. Anchored by Grace is dedicated to his memory, his passion for writing and to the promise that someday we would do it.

CHAPTER ONE

BIBLE VERSES

For unto us a Child is born, Unto us a Son is given; And the government will be upon His shoulder. And His name will be called Wonderful, Counselor, Mighty God, Everlasting Father, Prince of Peace. – Isaiah 9:6

My mom introduced me to God over breakfast: eggs, oatmeal, pancakes, and the words of Isaiah. He was her favorite prophet, maybe because Isaiah predicted the Messiah was coming, maybe because Isaiah predicted the gift Christ would bring with Him: God's grace. Each night Mom studied a different passage from her Bible, and each morning before school, we all gathered around her at our dark cherry-wood kitchen table so she could share that passage with us.

Her voice rang like a bell, and I hung on every sweet note: "'But He was wounded for our transgressions, He was bruised for our iniquities; the chastisement for our peace was upon Him, and by His stripes we are healed.' Isaiah 53:5."

In 1980, I was only 10, and I had little idea what transgressions, iniquities, or chastisement were, but Mom was good at making things make sense to us kids. She taught us it all meant something like this: "Isaiah knew Jesus hundreds of years before he was born.

He didn't know exactly who Jesus would be, but he knew a Messiah would be beaten, punished, and hated so the rest of us could be free."

"Free from what?" I asked.

"From the consequences of sin. Imagine, Keith, if you did something wrong, like cheating on a test at school, and the teacher was going to punish you, and you knew you deserved to be punished, but instead your brother stood up and told the teacher, 'Punish me instead!'"

It's not like we kids were saints or anything. If my mother said something like that to us, my big sister, Leslie, would most likely smirk at my big brother, Kyle. Leslie was two years older than me and already looked a lot like Mom, so a smirk looked pretty on her.

"What're you looking at?" Kyle was four years older than me, and he was the quiet one, so if he spoke up it was only to remind us he hated attention.

All Dad had to do was shoot Kyle a warning look and that would get everyone's attention. At our kitchen table, love and respect were unspoken rules.

"Why would Kyle want to be punished for something he didn't do?" My sister Julie was the baby, two years younger than me.

"Because y'all love each other." Mom was always the peacemaker.

"But Kyle's not even in my grade," I said, knowing it would make her laugh.

Oh, that laugh, how it made everyone smile. It wasn't just how musical it sounded, but that it was so full of love it engaged all of us in the discussion, made us all feel God's love so we could laugh along with her.

"So how did Isaiah know Jesus was coming?" I asked.

"Because God showed Isaiah visions of the future, so he could see Jesus' life happening in front of him, like a movie."

The way Mom talked about miracles and visions with her soft certainty, she made breakfast my favorite time of day. The way Dad smiled at her, I could tell he felt the same way.

***

My parents, Tom and Wanda, first started going together in ninth grade, in the small town of Conroe, Texas. Sometimes Mom teared up when she talked about those days, in a wistful way that made me wish I could go back in time and see it all: the first time he carried her books, the first time he defended her from a jerk on the playground, the first time he took her out for a burger after a Conroe High football game. Tom was a linebacker. Wanda was a cheerleader.

Dad said, "Your mom was always one of the nicest girls in school. She was a good friend to everyone she met."

"Your daddy looked like Elvis," Mom said. "He was voted most handsome in school."

Mom cried her eyes out when Dad went to Lamar University in Beaumont, Texas and she had to stay behind. Those first couple of years apart were too much for them, so they got married and she moved on campus with him while he finished his degree in chemical engineering. From that moment on, they never spent more than a day or two apart. After he graduated, they moved to Deerpark, Texas to start a family.

The way Mom and Dad looked at each other when I was growing up, I knew she still thought he looked like Elvis and he still thought she looked like a cheerleader. That didn't embarrass me the way some kids get embarrassed about their parents. Sitting at our kitchen table with one parent at either end, two of us kids on either side, made me feel safe, like God was watching them watching us.

***

In our house, and in God's house, I was my mother's son, but after school I reported to the garage, where my father took over. Dad spent years as a chemical engineer, but when I was in elementary school, he left that career to start a family business: Christian Enterprises. The Isbell Family became purveyors of religious knickknacks: clocks, framed pictures, and figurines etched with scriptures.

Dad assigned everyone in our family a job. He was responsible for production, creative strategies, and sales, while Mom kept the books and did whatever else was needed. My big brother and big sister were supposed to help with packing and mailing, but once Kyle hit high school he became less available, which led to shouting matches with our dad, which led to Dad banishing my brother to his room. So, Kyle wasn't much help.

My little sister and I worked in the garage, wadding newspaper to use as packing material to ship our products. Christian Enterprises was on a tight budget, and we couldn't afford packing bubbles or tissue, so Julie and I wadded ball after ball of paper and stuffed them into big black yard-bags. The garage door was always open so we were always either too hot or too cold, depending on the season.

My dad paid us by the bag, something like fifty cents each, so of course I wanted to fill each bag as fast as possible. We had an old clock in the garage, which Julie and I used to make a timed competition of it. We would each grab a bag, look up at the clock, wait until the minute hand hit the twelve—the clock didn't have a second hand—and shout, "Go!" Julie focused on wadding each ball to the exact shape and size Dad had instructed us, but I only focused on winning. Or so I thought. Dad periodically checked our work, and it seemed to me he always bypassed Julie and targeted me.

The first time, he walked straight up to my bag, pulled out a wad of paper, and said, "Son, this has got to be better quality. Remember, this has to protect the products we're sending to people, and to do that, it needs to be wadded up tighter to make more of a cushion." He pulled out one of Julie's. "See. Your sister has the right idea."

So, I rolled them tighter. Then he came back. "Oh boy, here we go… Let's inspect Keith's bag." He winked at Julie as he picked up one of the wads and said, "Looks better, but…"—here, he reached his arm straight down into my bag and pushed hard, leaning into it with his whole body, shoving the fluff of wadded paper all the way to the ground, "…now *that's* more like it."

The way he did it, I couldn't help but laugh. "Gee, thanks, Dad."

"You want to make money, you can't just do the minimum, Keith. You got to do more. I know you can work harder than that." He set a hand on my head, and that took the sting out of it.

I never felt angry with him about that sort of thing, and I never understood why Kyle got so ticked off in similar situations. I figured Dad just wanted me to be good at working so I could get a good job someday. But those were Kyle's teenage years, the years he took to complaining Dad always "hassled" him. This so-called "hassling" was a mystery to me, but then so was my brother's whole world, which soon included trucks, beer, and girls, while my whole world was still sports, sleepovers, and a daily dose of *The Flintstones*.

5

Whatever we kids were trying to figure out, Mom was always somewhere in the house, waiting with words of encouragement. Sometimes she would come to the garage and say, "Good job!" in case Dad forgot.

***

Every Christmastime, my mom read to us from a big, thick, antique book full of color illustrations. Whenever she wasn't reading it, that book sat displayed in a place of honor right next to our Christmas tree. It contained the story of the Nativity. I loved the story of Jesus' birth more than any other Bible tale. Maybe because it was all about how He was born dirt-poor, like we thought we were, and nobody knew He was destined to be a king.

But I believe the story my mom loved most of all was the story of Jesus' death. As much as I loved knowing He was born low and became great, she loved knowing He was born great but was brought low. She taught us that part of His greatness was letting that happen, though I was too young to understand it then.

When I was in middle school, our parents expected us kids to study Bible verses on our own, and to each make a presentation on one verse every morning. I was not a fan of this program, which no longer felt like storytelling but homework. How I hated homework. Still, I found ways to liven up the stories with jokes, sometimes mimicking our church minister—who had some odd twitches when he got ramped up in a sermon—until all of us were laughing.

Mom never got mad at me for that, just laughed along and said, "That's my little preacher."

She had called me that for as long as I could remember. We

had an old tape recording of me from when I was 7 or 8, and I was preaching the story about Joshua and the battle of Jericho. At one point I said, "…and the walls came tumbling down like little meatballs!" And my mom's contagious laugh bubbled up in the background. "That's my little preacher!" I loved making her laugh. It was my favorite sound in the world.

***

The year I started middle school was the year my parents moved us all back to their hometown of Conroe. Dad's new business was not taking off as fast as he hoped, so my parents found a cheaper house at the bottom of a winding dirt road in the woods. Every time it rained, the rain all ran downhill toward our place. The first year, the house flooded. We learned our lesson after that, and whenever a big storm hit, my father, Kyle and I would all brave the thunder and lightning and head out to dig a trench at the foot of our driveway. We'd be soaked to the bone, but at least our house wouldn't end up six inches deep in muddy rainwater.

I don't think we were poor, not exactly, but our life was humble for sure. Every chance we got, my brother and I loaded our rifles with buckshot, took our hound dog deep into the woods, and followed that dog until he treed a squirrel for us to shoot. Each trip we bagged several squirrels, carried them home, staked them out on an oak tree with two big nails in it, and skinned them. Then we gutted, boiled, and froze them. Every weekend, my mother took a few squirrels out of the freezer and stewed up a big pot of squirrel and dumpling. She served each of us a bowl of a squirrel stew, and set a tiny empty bowl next to that where we could drop any stray buckshot we bit into and had to spit out. My memory of Sunday night dinners consists of three sounds: conversation, laughter, and a little metallic, "plink, plink, plink."

There was only one other family that lived out there in the boonies, maybe a five- or ten-minute walk away, and nobody else for several miles. The father became my dad's business partner. They had three kids—two girls and a boy—and we all became friends. They were how I learned maybe we weren't poor, maybe my dad was just thrifty. Because these two men were partners in the same business, yet at the other house, their fridge boasted Coca-Cola, while ours only carried Big K cola, the Kroger brand. But my dad was my hero, so I never let that bother me, just teased him, "Hey, Dad, think you could hook me up with an A&W?"

Although our mom did the shopping, I'm sure the policy of buying off-brands was Dad's idea. He once said he couldn't see the point of using a different soap for our bodies than we used for our hair, so we used shampoo for both purposes. But even then, I never thought he was a tightwad, just worried about what would happen to all of us if the family business failed.

***

I'd always loved all sports—football, basketball, and especially baseball—and my father coached me in Little League. Dad liked to go for a run in the mornings, and I loved to go with him. In sixth grade, I started outrunning him, and that was an unexpected rush. I knew he wasn't letting me win, either. That's not how he was wired. Even when we played games as a family, he never babied us but encouraged us to keep trying, taught us if we worked hard we'd get better.

Dad usually drove me to middle school every day, and he liked to drop me off early so he could start his work day early.

In seventh grade, my first period was athletics, and Dad knew I liked running, so one day he asked, "Why don't you let me drop you off at 6:30? Then you can run a couple of miles before athletics."

"Sure, that sounds great!"

I didn't know he was going to make a habit of it. If I had, I still would have said yes, and not just because it was my dad asking. To me it wasn't a sacrifice, although it meant I missed hanging out with the other kids before class. I'd head to the empty locker room to change, then out to the track to run two miles before school. I loved having the track to myself. I took to running barefoot because I knew I could run faster with nothing between me and the earth.

After that I'd head straight to my athletics class. Sometimes the coach would start class by having us run a mile, and I'd already run two. I began to build more endurance than the other kids, consistently at the front of the pack. I'm sure my dad must have known that would happen, must have seen I had a gift and planned that before-school run as a way to develop it. Sure enough, I joined the track team and became obsessed with running, specifically long distance. I loved the simplicity of stepping on the track and knowing it didn't matter which athlete was popular, or who was the coach's favorite, or which kids' parents donated money to the team—knowing that whoever had the best speed and endurance would win.

The coach tried to get me to put on shoes, and I tried to wear them, but turned out it really did cut down my times, whether for psychological reasons or physical ones—maybe both. The coach just shrugged and let me go back to barefoot running.

Meanwhile, now that we kids were getting older and more self-sufficient, Mom took on leading the youth ministry at our small church, Faith Outreach.

That first year, in seventh grade, I started winning medals in one track event after another, especially the distance runs, until one day my mom said to me, "Hey, little preacher, I'm so proud of you, and I think my middle-school group at church would get a lot out of it if you'd talk to them about the idea of running to win."

"So, you want me to talk about how winning takes discipline and practice and stuff?"

"Yes, sure, but I'm talking more about a winning attitude."

"So, you want me to relate it to the Bible?"

"Of course. I see you, Keith, how much you light up when you're in the zone. That's what it's like when we're in sync with God. I want you to talk to the kids about that, about commitment, passion, and follow-through, about making up your mind to do the hard thing, about knowing you can win if God is with you."

She knew I thought that way because those were lessons she had taught me. My dad was all about figuring out the practical steps to achieve goals, but my mom was all about finding the mental and spiritual mindset to yield a winning attitude. When Dad gave me advice about running, he talked about daily practice, cross-training, focusing on my breathing, strategies to improve endurance, the power of pushing through pain, and more. But from the beginning, my mom had talked about running with God, how if I prayed and had faith and brought the best of myself to my running, or to anything I did, then I could perform miraculous feats.

I felt so proud my mom thought I had what it took to speak to her group that it never occurred to me to think of it as an extra chore or as something I might be too nervous to do. At an age when most kids are terrified to get caught being different, I thought it was fun to reveal my secrets: how I thought and felt about running and winning, what I did to prepare physically, but more importantly what I did to prepare mentally.

"You've got to believe," I told my mother's youth group. "You've got to believe the guy to the left and the guy to the right are no better than you. Or if they are, that doesn't matter, let them be better. The only person I need to be 'better than' is me. I just need to be the best of myself." My mom helped me connect that to Jesus, how He helped me be the best of myself.

The way my mother smiled at me while I talked was similar to the way I looked at myself in the mirror after a big win. That's when I understood: she saw herself in me. I knew my mother loved all of us kids equally, but I realized she saw in me her ability to tell a story that could change the way people thought about things. I caught a glimpse of it too, when a couple of kids laughed and nodded in recognition at the parts of my story where I described a moment when I thought I was going to lose but instead turned things around. For a moment I thought, "I *am* Mom's little preacher." Not that I wanted to be a minister, but I sure liked talking to people.

My freshman year of high school, my mom sat me down and said, "They're not going to let you run barefooted anymore. You know that."

"Yeah, I know, the coach told me the rules require shoes. But I was wondering…is there any rule about what kind of shoes?"

"I'm listening…"

I suggested we make a pair of crew socks look like shoes. Her face lit up. She asked me to get her my newest socks, and then she got to work: cut them down the middle from the ankle to the tops of my toes, punched holes on either side for laces, and stitched in duct tape on the bottom. For the finishing touch, I found a magic marker, and drew a Nike swish on the sides.

The coach let me get away with it. Then we went to a district meet where we were up against a school with a legendary track team: the local dynasty. I went up to the starting line for the two-mile. Maybe three other guys in their lineup were runners to watch for. One of them had the two-mile record for the State of Texas. It did not occur to me to even bother competing with him, but I figured I had a chance to get second, maybe third, and pick up points for my team. As we all stretched and shook out the jitters, the starter walks up and gives my feet a long hard look. He walked away and came back with a judge.

"Man, what are you doing?" the judge asked.

"What do you mean?" I asked, though I knew exactly what he meant.

"You have to wear shoes to run."

"These are my shoes."

The starter said, "Those aren't shoes. They're socks."

The other runners had all gone quiet, a few staring, a few looking away.

"They're shoes," I said, and started to point out the features. "They've got laces, they've got heels, they even have a swooshy design."

"Which you drew on there!"

"Well, define a shoe." I was truly not trying to be rebellious. I wanted to run, and I believed the more natural the contact between my feet and the ground, the better I ran.

They could not figure out how to refute my arguments as to what constituted a shoe, so they gave in. "All right," the judge said. "You can run."

The starter fired his pistol, and I bolted off the line. The opposing team went out of their way to target me, boxed me in, and one kid waited until we were far into the course, too far out for any judges to see, and then he spiked me on the back of the legs. Still I finished third. I felt proud of my run. I'd given it my all, I'd beaten most of the field against tough odds, and I'd bumped our team up in the standings—all worthy wins in my book.

Then, as soon as the race ended, the judge walked over to me. "You're disqualified."

"For what?!" I was still pumped with adrenaline from the run and from my victory, and I couldn't hide my dismay at the unfairness of this sudden change.

"You stepped on the inside line seven times."

I was too flabbergasted to figure out how to respond to such an obvious lie from an adult. I knew better than to step on the inside line, so I always kept it in sight, especially when opponents tried to box me in. Even if I had lost sight of the line, there was no way I'd done so seven times. I knew this was about me outsmarting them over the shoes, about me embarrassing an adult in front of a bunch of kids, about power and control. I gave up pretty quick. I was a poor kid from the woods, and the other team was the local dynasty. I knew how this would go.

My coach, on the other hand, came completely unglued. "That's total B.S. and you know it. You can't take this away from this young man!"

But they did. I never forgot that moment. I never forgot that I set a new personal best for the two-mile: 10:17, which was twenty seconds faster than my previous record. I never forgot that doing one's best sometimes means trying a new way to do things. And I never forgot how much that threatens some people. I never ran with my self-made shoes again. My sophomore year, I switched to spikes like everyone else. I never ran that fast again. This wasn't a fight I was eager to take on. I just loved to run, just me and that track and God, seeing how fast I could go.

***

In 1984, the year I turned 14, my parents did something they had never done before. They lied to us kids, lied, by saying nothing at all. One day, they sat us down in our living room and told us some bad news: Mom had been diagnosed with pancreatic cancer. That part was true. Then Dad said, "No matter what the doctors say, we are going to beat this. So, we don't want you to worry. With a little help from her doctors and a lot of faith in the Lord, we believe your mom will be healed by the stripes of Jesus."

That sort of absolute assurance contradicted what the doctor had told them. He had made it clear that, with this type of cancer, there was no hope. All they could do was make my mother as comfortable as possible. They did not even recommend chemotherapy. Back in 1984, pancreatic cancer was a death sentence. But they didn't tell us that part.

My parents were honest people, and I don't believe they were purposely misleading us or trying to give us false hope. Maybe they only heard the parts of the doctor's prognosis that they wanted to hear. Or maybe they believed what they wanted to believe: that the sort of miracles God performed in the Bible might shine on our house. Maybe they were trying to protect us from things they thought it would not help us to know. We kids sure needed to believe what they said was true.

Sitting around our kitchen table, where Mom had taught all of us the importance of faith, I took everything she and Dad told us as gospel. As far as I was concerned, Mom was going to get medical treatment, we were all going to pray a lot, and everything was going to be okay.

Mom was going to run to win, just like she'd taught me.

CHAPTER TWO

A NEW HAIRCUT

"'Behold, I cry, "Violence!" but I get no answer; I shout for help,
but there is no justice.'" – Job 19:7

The months that followed my mom's diagnosis were brutal. As
much as Mom believed in running to win, she tumbled downhill
fast. Within three months she looked like a different person. I told
myself it was from chemotherapy. She went to the doctor sometimes, and she took some kind of pills, but what kind of medicine
it was I didn't know. Maybe chemo, maybe painkillers. I thought
sometimes I heard her cry out in the night, like she was in pain.
Whatever the medication was, I figured it wasn't working very well.

Through it all, as she lost so much weight her clothes hung on
her, as the circles under her eyes darkened, as the shadow over her
grew long, she and Dad never changed their story: Mom was going to get well. She refused to listen to any doubtful talk, insisted
we remain positive because God could conquer anything through
our faith.

"Yeah, I've got cancer, but I'm going to beat this," she said, but
her voice sounded faded, like she was talking to us over a radio
station far away.

Six months after her diagnosis, November was upon us, and as we got ready for the feasts of the holidays, she lost her appetite. She was rail thin, but her belly began to swell. At one point, I might have even fantasized she was pregnant, because I could more easily imagine Mom and Dad wanting to surprise us with that sort of news than I could imagine them hiding from us that she was riddled with an unstoppable cancer.

I knew things were serious when she stopped going to church. The only thing Mom loved as much as her family was God, and her favorite place to go was church. I had never known her to miss a service, even if she wasn't feeling well, unless she had something contagious. But I knew cancer wasn't contagious.

On Thanksgiving, she had no energy to get up, so we served her turkey and stuffing in bed. She fell asleep, the plate still waiting by her bedside barely touched. Why was she getting worse? She did everything she was supposed to do: went to the doctor, prayed, kept a positive attitude. If only she would eat, I thought, she'd get stronger.

One Sunday before Christmas the rest of us went to church and, as usual, the pastor listed those congregation members who were on his prayer list. I jolted to attention when he said, "Wanda Isbell has terminal cancer. Let's pray for her and the Isbell family as they face this trial." Terminal? What did he mean? I looked to my father, but he had already closed his eyes to pray. I looked around the pews. A few people looked our way, a mouth covered, tears in someone's eyes, a quiet gasp from another—stunned because they didn't know. My mother had asked us not to tell anyone. Until that moment, none of them knew for sure what was wrong with her, though many must have guessed. She looked so bad. But they all knew Wanda, and they all loved her. I felt the power of that love, like electricity filling the room, as more than a hundred people all bowed their heads to pray.

I didn't lower my head. I was too busy thinking: wait a minute, *terminal*? Who says it's terminal? Mom and Dad said it was going to be okay. The doctor said it would be okay. The cancer is curable. She's getting treatment. It's just chemotherapy making her sick. Right? Except Mom never talked about chemo. Was she even getting chemo?

I stared at my father's bowed head. He was the only one who could have told the pastor to ask for prayers. Did he say that word to the pastor: *terminal*? If anyone knew what was going on, Dad would. Maybe the pastor was one of those guys who didn't understand cancer was no longer a death sentence, not in modern times. He probably made a mistake.

I refused to bow my head and pray for my mom like she was terminal, like she was dying, because that would be like saying he was right. I refused to say that word to God until I first heard it from Mom. I knew she would never lie to me. I knew Dad wouldn't either. Why would they say one thing to the pastor and lead their own kids to believe something different?

When I got home, I went to her room, and sat on the edge of the bed, careful not to jiggle the mattress, because I knew that hurt her, because she always flinched a little if I did. "Mom, pastor said today that you're sick and that this is terminal. He said you're not going to beat this like you said." I was afraid to look at her.

She reached a hand to my face, and I saw the effort it took her. She left her hand there, waiting for me to look her in the eyes. "Don't listen to him. I'm going to be okay, and don't listen to anyone who says otherwise. Don't listen to that kind of talk." It was the strongest I had heard her voice in months, and her eyes said she was telling the truth. But what did she mean? She said she was *going to be okay*, but she didn't say she was *going to live*.

I would never in a million years call my mother a liar. But at that moment, I felt a space open between us, in the place where we used to talk to each other. Now we couldn't talk because I knew she was holding something back. Still, I trusted what her eyes said, that she wasn't lying about all of it, wasn't lying about her unwavering faith that she was going to be okay.

***

We moved her bed into the living room. "I can't miss my favorite time of year," she said. "I want to be surrounded by my family for Christmas." She did not say, "…for my last Christmas." She didn't have to. By then my mom, who was about five-foot-four weighed maybe 85 pounds, and nearly half that must have been excess fluid pooling in her abdomen. At 15, I didn't yet know that when a body shuts down, fluid gathers in the liver, kidneys, and pancreas.

Mom's skin and eyes turned yellow.

Christmas morning, we opened presents around her bed. By then, she could barely speak above a whisper, so she asked me to read the Nativity Story from the big antique book. I did my best, though I stumbled a lot.

"That's my little preacher," she said.

"He's not so little anymore," Dad said.

"None of them are," Mom said.

As I read, she asked me to hold up the book and show her each and every color illustration, which she devoured with her eyes. The only feast she could manage to eat. She could not digest food anymore.

With Mom's remaining strength, she insisted we not sit by her bed all day, said it was enough to be in the center of the room, to watch us come and go, but that we must get out and enjoy the holidays. So, on New Year's Eve, I planned to go to a party at a friend's house. My hair was getting so long my bangs were in my eyes. I didn't mind long hair, but I was starting to look like a hippie, and that wasn't my look. I had ignored it at first, but now my hair was hanging in my eyes making it hard to see. I knew it needed cutting, but Mom had always cut my hair, my whole life, and I could hardly ask her.

I thought about asking my big sister, Leslie, but I couldn't bring myself to do it. It would be like admitting defeat, admitting my mom was no longer who she used to be, admitting she was too weak to be our mom anymore. So, the morning of New Year's Eve, I holed up in the bathroom with a pair of scissors and cut my own hair for the first time. I didn't know what to do when I got to the back. I tried holding up a hand mirror, but I couldn't do that and cut at the same time. I gave up, took my best aim, and hacked it off. I held up the hand-mirror and tried to check it, but I couldn't get a good angle. I stared at myself in the mirror, and the guy who looked back at me looked mad. "Screw it!" I said to that guy, and walked out of there, no idea if my hair was all crooked or what.

On my way out, I walked over to Mom's bed to kiss her goodbye.

"Come here," she said, beckoning me to lean down.

So, I did.

She reached up a hand and played with my bangs, ran her fingers through the hair on top of my head. She chuckled. "You cut your hair."

"Yeah. I know I messed it all up." I felt guilty, like she might think cutting my own hair was some sort of accusation against her, like me not asking her to do it indicated some failing on her part, like that haircut meant I no longer had faith in her or her God.

"No, you did a good job. You always do." She riffled my hair. "You look handsome, Keith, just like your daddy."

That was the moment I knew. She was letting go.

That was the last time I talked to her.

***

Sometime between the New Year's Eve party I went to that night and our family gathering for breakfast on New Year's Day, my mom fell into a coma. It was like she had waited just long enough to ring in the holidays with us, just long enough to send us off into one more year, and then she couldn't wait anymore. It didn't happen fast though, at least not fast enough—not to my way of thinking.

For five days, we listened to my mom struggle for each breath.

For five days, I prayed, "Take her. If you're real, God, if you exist, don't do this to her."

For five days, our house filled with people, coming and going, all gathering around my mom in the living room, whispering in her ear like they were entrusting her with their final secrets, secrets she would now take to her grave. I imagined many of her friends thought of her the way many Catholics think of their saints, like an intermediary so close to God they knew they could trust her with their burdens, knew she would understand and assure them of God's forgiveness. Now they wanted to be there for her too, but it all seemed too late. Could she hear them? Could she feel how much she was loved by a whole town? Many of the people who came had been friends with her since high school. She never made a single enemy in Conroe.

After folks talked to her, they murmured to each other like my mom was already gone. I wished most of them would leave so she could die in peace and quiet with just her husband and kids around her. But I didn't know who I would send away if I could: her sister who grew up with her? My grandmother, Maw Maw, who was her own mother? Her oldest friend, who used to make her giggle so hard I could almost imagine they were still cheerleaders when they sat talking over coffee? I guessed Mom would have been happy to know they all came. I was the one who needed to be alone. Needed the chaos to stop. Needed things to stop moving so fast.

Around suppertime, my stomach was growling with hunger. The kitchen was full of food my parents' friends had brought, casserole dishes stacked everywhere, full of soft, comforting foods like cheese and pasta and cornbread. But I couldn't bear the thought of eating. Not when my mom couldn't.

She hadn't eaten a bite for days, yet her stomach continued to grow. I thought it was the cancer growing and I wanted to push my hand against it, to crush it, to make it stop. I ran to the bathroom and locked the door, prayed again. "Why won't you take her? What kind of God would do this to someone when all she ever did was love you?"

That's about the time I heard my dad scream, "Oh, Lord!"

I ran out of the bathroom. He was holding her up, like maybe if he held her higher God might bring her back, or like maybe if he held her tight she might stay a moment longer. But she was gone. Her body limp in his arms and him wailing in a way I did not want to hear, because if a guy as strong and smart as my dad couldn't figure out how to bear this, how could the rest of us? My aunt sat on the bed with her head on my mom's leg, crying.

I had thought death might bring peace, but the room seemed more chaotic than ever. There were maybe fifteen people in the house: my dad, my aunt, my grandmother, another aunt, us four kids. After she passed, a bunch more people showed up, I have no idea who.

I hit the ground, crawled behind the couch, and cried like a little kid. I'd never been through anything like this. None of us had. My mother had taught me about heaven all her life, but so far everything about this was hell and I couldn't see past it.

After a while, two or three strangers came in, placed her body on a stretcher, and wheeled her out. It was strange to see her so silent and still when I always thought of her as joyful and giggling. I think that was the first time I looked around for my siblings.

Kyle, who was 18, grabbed his Bible from his room and took it outside to the porch. He refused to come back inside until everyone outside our immediate family left. I went to the front door to see what he was doing, and he wasn't reading that Bible at all. I knew he was holding it because Mom had given it to him, because it was the place she went for answers, but she wasn't here—and who could tell us what this all meant without her?

My sisters were in their room, Leslie holding Julie, smoothing her hair the way Mom might have done. I envied them. This wasn't the kind of thing brothers did, at least not Kyle and me.

That night, after everyone left, Dad pulled all of us kids into my sisters' room, and said, "Starting today, I'll be your dad *and* your mom, and I'm going to do the best I can for you guys." That was all he could manage to say before he fell into an awkward silence.

Without any discussion, as if our next move had already been decided, all of us, including Dad, shuffled out to the living room and lay down on the floor, to sleep next to Mom's now-empty bed. Kind of like a litter of motherless puppies all piled together. Nobody wanted to sleep in their own rooms. Certainly not my dad.

My mom passed on January 5, 1985. She was 43. She was the rock that held our family together, like a keystone in a church. Who would keep us from falling apart now?

CHAPTER THREE

THE ATHEIST

For my thoughts are not your thoughts, neither are your ways
my ways, declares the Lord. – Isaiah 55:8

After I prayed for God to end my mother's suffering and be done with it, I decided never to speak to Him again. Sure, He answered my prayer, but in my opinion, he took His sweet time about it, and I couldn't forgive Him for that. Worse, I couldn't understand it. I could not believe a kind and loving God, the kind of God my Mother had devoted heart and soul to, would allow such a thing if it were in His power to stop it. I was convinced He was either cruel or didn't exist. Either way, I was so enraged I wanted nothing to do with Him.

"God's not real," I said to anyone I thought might listen. At 14, I understood the existence of God was something nobody had the power to either prove or disprove. I knew Christianity was about faith and the decision to either have it or not. I didn't have it. It seemed to me my father tried to hang on to his faith and, from my bitter teenage perspective, this was what caused him to suffer beyond endurance. His wife had been the person he counted on to help him make decisions and bear life's burdens. Throughout my childhood, after bedtime, I used to fall asleep to the murmurs of my mom and dad in the kitchen, and those sounds told me all our problems were being taken care of, either by them as a team, or by the Lord they leaned on.

After Mom passed, the one person Dad had left to lean on was his own father. They had always been close, and in those difficult days they grew closer. Pats on the back changed to great big bear-hugs, in which my father found comfort leaning on his father's shoulders. Instead of Mom and Dad's voices murmuring me to sleep, I now fell asleep to the deep voices of two strong men. Yes, my father was weakened by grief, but his father was shoring him up until he grew strong again. It left a small hope kindling in me that someday my dad might be for me what his dad was for him, that their strength in hard times might be a legacy that could be passed down.

Then, one month after my mom died of cancer, my grandfather, who had been fighting his own cancer, also died. The way I saw it, my grandpa's fighting spirit had been the only thing holding my dad together, giving him the strength to hold the rest of us together. Once Grandpa died, that all unraveled, leaving nobody to keep us from falling apart. To me, this validated my decision to no longer believe in a heavenly Father.

Dad made Leslie, Julie, and me keep going to church with him. I went along because I couldn't bear for Dad to feel like he'd lost a son on top of everyone else. I said nothing to him about losing my faith. I knew he would say something about what Mom would have wanted, and what was the point of worrying about that anymore? But whenever I could come up with any excuse—I needed to go to the bathroom, I felt sick, I had promised to help a friend with something—I skipped out of church early or altogether. As for Kyle, he no longer lived at home, and he never came to church with us anymore.

Dad often went out of town on business, networking with fellow entrepreneurs and attending meetings of the Christian Booksellers Association, seeking support and advice to keep our family business going. It didn't help. Business slowed way down. Like my dad, Christian Enterprises was fading. He stopped asking my sisters and me to help with packing, shipping, and bookkeeping. He started interviewing for other jobs. "Just keeping my options open," he would say, or something like it. My brother, Kyle, was one of the few people who continued to work for him—which might have been part of the problem.

Kyle had gone off to college before Mom died. After she died, he dropped out, but he didn't come home then either. Instead he lived all over, sleeping on a couch at this friend's house, renting an apartment with that friend, or renting a whole house with a bunch of buddies.

My older sister, Leslie, was a high school senior, and she took on many of the motherly tasks Mom used to do: cooking our breakfasts, packing our lunches, telling Julie and me to do our homework.

I would say, "I already did my homework," even though I'd barely arrived home, or "I don't have any," even though I did.

My sister was onto me. "Mom wouldn't want you staying out all night. She'd want you to work hard at school."

"Mom's dead," I'd say. "She doesn't want anything anymore."

That shut Leslie up right quick. I felt bad seeing her fight tears, but I never felt bad enough to change my attitude. I took perverse pleasure in pointing out Mom was just plain gone, not in some heavenly place where she smiled down on me and continued to inspire me to greatness. Now and then I tried to be a good kid, for Leslie, as if she were Mom's living conscience left behind to keep us on the right path. More often I ignored her. Part of me wanted Leslie to fail at mothering us because I couldn't stand the idea of my mother being replaced, not even by my sister, who was as beautiful as our mom with the same sweet spirit. Sometimes it was painful to look at her.

Kyle came home on rare visits, to borrow money from Dad or grab a meal because he was short on cash, though he never admitted that was why. On one of those visits, he and I sat on the porch together in silence. Dinner had been pretty silent too, other than when we said grace or when Kyle goaded Dad into the usual argument about how Kyle was wasting his God-given brains, wasting his God-given life.

I murmured, so Dad wouldn't hear, "Doesn't it feel phony to you now, all this praying, all this talk about God. Like why did we ever bother?"

Kyle looked at me like I had spit on Mom's grave. "Why do you say that? Because Mom died? Don't forget John 3:16: 'For God so loved the world that He gave His only begotten Son, that whoever believes in Him should not perish but have everlasting life.'"

"That doesn't explain why God tortured her before he gave her everlasting life."

"Mom wouldn't have seen it that way. She would have said we just can't always understand God's ways because we can't see the whole picture like He can."

"You can't tell me there's some big plan that required our mom, who never did anything to hurt a soul, to go through all that pain."

"I'm not trying to convince you of anything. I'm just surprised. I mean, you're the little preacher, not me."

He was right. I wasn't sure why I was talking to him about my newfound atheism. Maybe because he didn't go to church with us anymore, or because he ran around getting drunk with his friends. I guess I thought he might see it the way I did, because he sure didn't act very Godly. But he neither approved nor disapproved. He was baffled. I guess I mostly told him because I wanted to tell somebody the life I'd known was over, and I sure couldn't tell Dad. He had enough on his plate.

Leslie caught part of the conversation and grew defensive. "Mom would be so disappointed if she knew you used her death as an excuse to turn your back on God. She'd never do that!"

"Don't you see? That's why it doesn't make sense. She never turned her back on Him, but He turned His back on her anyway. Why would He do that?"

"Maybe to test our faith."

"Or maybe there's a simpler answer: He never turned His back on her because He never existed in the first place."

"You're wrong."

Leslie talked about Bible characters who kept their faith in God despite terrible trials, like Job who praised God through a multitude of undeserved punishments, Stephen the martyr who sang God's praises even as he was stoned to death, David who gave thanks to God after his young son died. To me those stories proved nothing except that the Bible's authors worshipped a cruel God, which made me all the more relieved to believe He didn't exist.

My younger sister, Julie, wasn't in on these conversations, or much of anything. She was the baby, and we either ignored her or did everything for her. If she was lost in the shuffle, then so were we all. None of us had a mother anymore. Why should she be any different?

***

Not long after his wife and his father died, my dad started dating a totally weird woman from out of state. He ran into some good friends at a conference of the Christian Booksellers Association, and they offered to set him up with this woman. "She's perfect for you," they promised. Everything was going wrong in his life, and no doubt their hearts were in the right place, so I guess he figured, "Why not?" He drove to Missouri so his friends could introduce this "perfect woman." She looked perfect on the outside all right, a 38-year-old former Gloria Vanderbilt model. As for what she was like on the inside, she acted pretty excited about Dad's Christian business, which seemed to imply she was a good Christian.

I think Dad might have misrepresented the value of his business to Trixie—that's not her name, but it fits the way I remember her so I'll call her that. His overstated success as an entrepreneur might be why the Gloria Vanderbilt model got more excited about him than his aging-football-hero good looks seemed to call for, especially considering the little cloud of sorrow that rained on him wherever he went.

He didn't bring Trixie around to meet us kids at first. This made sense to us because she lived in Missouri, so he only saw her sporadically. He talked about her, so we knew she existed. We didn't know how long he'd been seeing her when they got engaged, but it couldn't have been more than a few times in a few months because it had only been about a year since our mom's death. But he decided it was time to bring his fiancée home to meet the family.

"Aren't you all just a-dooooor-a-ble!" Trixie shrieked when she saw us, like we were contestants at a beauty pageant for toddlers instead of a pack of surly teenagers.

Our eyes about popped out of our heads. The easiest way to explain our reaction: she was hot. Trixie was the epitome of 1980s excess: big sprayed-stiff hair, big layers of makeup, big smile, and tight jeans. She looked like she'd had work done even though she wasn't yet 40.

This only made it all the weirder when, upon Dad announcing their engagement, she told us: "I want y'all to know I'm a Christian woman who has been saving myself for the right man."

We stared at her, puzzled.

"I mean I'm a virgin."

It was all we could do to wait until she left before we burst out laughing.

"Who *says* that?" Leslie said.

"Are you fucking kidding me?" Kyle said.

"What does she mean?" Julie asked.

"What are we supposed to say?" I said. "'Wow, okay, sorry to hear that'?"

I knew what we were all thinking: How can our father replace the most devoted wife and mother in the world with this cardboard cutout of a woman?

It seemed to me like almost no time passed before I was pulling at my collar at their wedding, feeling like I was choking. It was her first marriage, so she had to have a big white wedding with all the trimmings. I felt nauseous eating this woman's sugary white cake with buttercream flowers when I knew Mom would have hated everything about her, knew Dad would never have given her the time of day if he'd been in his right mind.

Dad never said to us, "This is your new mother." But, to me, it was bad enough that this woman slept in the bed that used to be my mom's.

***

I continued my trip off the rails while Trixie's behavior grew more and more bizarre. I skipped classes by day, stayed out drinking all night. Everybody knew I had gone from Mom's Little Preacher to The Devil's Playmate, but nobody said anything to me, until Trixie decided it was time for us to have a little talk. She swept into my bedroom, took my hands dramatically in hers, and, eyes filled with tears that never smeared her perfect waterproof mascara, wailed how she saw that I was a suffering soul and wanted to pray over me. She looked and sounded like an acute whack-job.

I wanted to say, "You're the problem with Christianity, a hypocrite who's all appearance and no substance." Instead, I muttered something like, "Thank you, but not right now," and walked away.

One time I was taking a shower in the main bath. It was one of those bathrooms with two sections: an inner area with a shower and toilet, and an outer area with two sinks. Both doors were closed, the door to the outer sinks and the door to the inner shower and toilet. But I came out of the shower, wet and naked, to find her standing in the outer part of the bathroom by the sinks, holding my towel, staring into space. I did not get the impression she was coming on to me or anything like that. It was obvious she wasn't aware of where she was or why she was there.

"What're you doing?" I asked.

She shook her head like she was trying to wake herself. "Here. Here's the towel," she said, as if she had been waiting all along for me to finish showering so she could hand me my towel like a servant.

I never told my father about that moment, or the many other weird moments like it, because I feared it would upset him, or that he would explain it away, which seemed worse. But I told my brother, and we agreed, "This woman is half nuts!" No doubt the thought occurred to her too: "What am I doing, living in the woods with a depressed widower who owns a business that's circling the drain and has three angry kids who hate me? I must be half nuts!"

Although I'd given up on God, I tried to hold on to the compassion my mother taught me, and at odd moments I felt sorry for Trixie. I could tell she was depressed. But at the tail end of every charitable thought always came this one: "Whatever your problems are, lady, I'm sorry, but why make the rest of us suffer with you? Get the hell out of our home!"

I never did anything she told me to do. If she said, "Go cut the grass," I walked past her as if she weren't there.

"Show some respect," Dad said.

"She's not my mom," I said.

Before anybody could think of a retort to that old chestnut, I was out the door.

Trixie was the opposite of my mother. My mom was beautiful inside and out, but this woman was superficial and materialistic. She spent money Dad didn't have on clothes, makeup, and household conveniences.

Although she could act outgoing when she worked herself into a frenzy, half the time she was so drugged she couldn't keep her eyes open. She lay on the couch all the time. She didn't bother trying to hide her bottles of painkillers. "I have a bad back," she complained, and I believe she did. But she was always loopy. It didn't take us kids long to figure out she was an addict, though I don't think my dad had any idea.

***

Trixie must have deduced, not long after she moved into our house in the sticks, that our swaybacked beds and couches, scratch-and-dent tables, and cheap knickknacks were not a sign of simple country tastes but of a working-class income. Once she realized her husband was not an up-and-coming entrepreneur, she became plain old-fashioned mean, treated him like he was a piece of gum stuck to her shoe. She never smiled at him.

After years of listening to my mom build my dad up after hard days: "It'll be all right, honey… I know you'll make the right decision… You're a good man, I trust you…"—it was painful to hear Trixie talk to him like he was an obstacle in her way. If he didn't respond instantly to one of her demands for something she wanted him to do or buy, she would blink at him and then slowly repeat whatever she had just said: "What…I…told…you…is…" Like he was too stupid to understand.

My dad never lost his temper or called her on her condescending attitude. Maybe because he had gotten into the habit of kindness with my mom. Maybe because his first partnership had been built on authentic love, and he couldn't stand to admit that all he had with Trixie was physical infatuation and underneath that, there was nothing at all.

Trixie's perspective seemed clear to me: she had thought he had money, and when she found out he didn't, she blamed him. I knew my dad was lonely, but I felt like Trixie was making it worse, by providing a stark contrast to what he had lost. He had lost his soul mate, and now he was stuck with a self-centered pill-head who didn't love him. Neither of them were getting what they wanted.

I don't know what Dad's business was worth when he and Trixie met. Maybe it really was going as well as he told her it was. But that ended fast. It wasn't clear if his business went downhill because he emotionally tanked after Mom's death, or because she was no longer around to help him manage things, or because he just wasn't into it anymore. Maybe it was just bad luck. Whatever the reason, he sold the business to somebody who lived two hours away in another small town.

After that, he found a job selling insurance. He came home less and less. He always had a great work ethic, but more than that I think he didn't want to come home. Not to see Trixie, but also not to see us, not to see the empty space nobody talked about, the space where Mom used to sit and laugh, tell us about God's love, and reassure us all was right with the world.

Dad and Trixie were married less than a year when, one day while he was gone and we kids were at school, her parents pulled a moving van up to our house and carried out most of our furniture: couches, chairs, tables, beds, most of it stuff we had owned before Trixie came. By the time I came home from cross-country practice, they were already gone. The front yard was full of holes, from the weight of all our furniture I guess. She took a lot of small valuables too, many of them wedding gifts, not from Trixie's wedding but my mother's: plates, glasses, silverware.

I walked into my dad's bedroom, too dumbfounded to speak. Every last thing was gone aside from his clothes: the bed, the dresser, the nightstands, the lamps. So, I went to my room, tore my bed down, and put it back together in his room. Then I dragged my dresser in there, all by myself, so he wouldn't have to walk into an empty room when he came home. Later, he walked into my room and saw that all I had on the floor was a sheet and blanket.

"Keith, you can't just sleep on the floor."

"Of course I can. I can sleep anywhere. I know we'll get more furniture at some point."

"Thank you, son." I could hear the tears stuck in his throat.

My dad still talks about that sometimes, how much it meant to him that I did that. All I could think was, *How much more can this guy handle?*

Trixie later had the audacity to call my brother and say, "I left my perfume in the bathroom. Would you mind sending it to me?"

I told my brother, "I'm going to empty out her nasty little bottle of stinking perfume, piss in it, and then send it to her."

He laughed.

"I'm serious," I said. "Let's do it!"

Kyle ran to tell our dad, who charged into the bathroom. "Don't even think about it! That is not how we do things." He packed the perfume in a box, with little wads of paper carefully stuffed around it to make sure it didn't break, like the wads of paper I used to put around the little curios he sold for Christian Enterprises. And he mailed it to her.

CHAPTER FOUR

THE BEER FEST COMMITTEE

Wine is a mocker, strong drink a brawler, and whoever is led astray by it is not wise. – Proverbs 20:1

I was never a great student, but when my mom was alive I used to try my best because I never wanted to disappoint her. My report cards looked like flyers for restaurants where C's were on special, but when I got the occasional A or B, Mom gave me an extra hug. After she died, the hugs died with her. I started getting D's and F's. I had always been a star runner, and when Mom was alive I believed "running to win" was all about faith. Sometimes I felt closer to God on a track than in a church. After she died, "running to win" just reminded me she had lost. When Mom was alive I tried to be kind to everyone like she was. After she died, I stopped being Mr. Nice Guy, and decided to be Mr. Fun Guy.

I used to be Mom's Little Preacher, but now all I preached was a good time. Mom was dead, so God didn't exist and being a good son didn't matter anymore.

It was not just my father's ex-wife Trixie I had no patience for. I had no patience for my dad, my family, my church, my school, for the life I used to live when my mother still lived. I didn't know this was grief. If Mom were around she might have talked me through

35

it. As it was, I zoned out. Quit cross-country, the track team, sports of any kind. Stopped turning in homework. Stopped coming home. Started roaming the night with my buddies. Started getting drunk every night. Started doing whatever it took to break the rules. I became popular, for all the wrong reasons.

Denying God felt liberating at first, an exercise of free will, permission to do anything I wanted. Junior year, my last period was English with Miss Cook, who was older than God. I would wait for her to take attendance, and the moment her back was turned, I'd open a window, climb out, and take off. Nobody ever narked me out. The class snickered silently as I left, then went poker-faced when she turned their way. They acted like they were members of my exciting club, like we had a secret together and that made us cool. "That was hilarious, man!" they'd say if they saw me in the halls, though more often I was nowhere on campus to be found.

Miss Cook filled out her grade-book in pencil, and sometimes she left the class unsupervised. One day I moseyed up to the book, opened it to my name, erased my bad grades, and gave myself better ones. Not all A's, or she might notice. Then again, maybe she did. Miss Cook was only a couple of years from retirement, and surely, I wasn't the first teenager she had seen try to stick it to his teachers. Maybe she figured why bother? I got a C in her class, but I failed all the others.

Younger teachers who still wanted to be heroes, to reach unreachable kids, had heartfelt talks with me. My school counselor, Mr. Green, said, "Keith, I know things have been rough at home." That kind of ticked me off, him talking like he knew me. But I gave him my best Little Preacher smile, said it was nothing I couldn't handle, and promised to try harder. The promises never lasted. Trying was hard. I wanted easy.

***

I think I was over at my friend Daryll's house, drinking beer with a bunch of guys in his room, the first time someone passed me a joint. I was in an "I'll try anything once" frame of mind at all times, so I took a couple of hits. Next thing I knew, I couldn't move, frozen into a beat-up easy chair. It felt like I was trapped in a room full of strangers, with me the biggest stranger of all. I decided I did not like marijuana. Decided I was a beer man. Beer was easy.

Junior and senior year, a handful of my drinking buddies and I put our love of beer to work for us. We started a club called the BFC. I made up the acronym, thinking it would keep our purpose a secret from adults: BFC, Beer Fest Committee. I don't think we fooled anyone. We appointed ourselves as BFC officers, with me as president and my friends as vice president, secretary, and treasurer. Our mission: Become the go-to guys for partying in Conroe.

Conroe was a little big town, with a population of about 10,000, but we were surrounded by a lot of small towns, all crawling with bored teens. Conroe High was the spoke of the wheel on which Montgomery County turned. The stadium was named after a guy my dad had played football with. Everybody knew everybody. Everybody was a redneck and proud of it. And the boys of the BFC provided the beer to lubricate them all.

Our BFC crew would rove the far reaches of town in search of open land: an abandoned lot, a clearing in the woods, a creek down by the factories. Then we'd hire a band, pay some friends a few bucks to run security, and ask others to bring wood for a bonfire. The key piece, without which the rest would never have worked: my brother Kyle was 21 and our source for bottomless kegs of beer. How else could I declare myself president without anybody pausing to question my authority? In return for buying the beer, Kyle received a cut of our profits.

Of course, there were profits. My mom might have taught me the power of God, but my dad taught me the power of matching the right product to the right audience. I knew Christians liked Bibles and baubles with scriptures on them, and I knew high school kids liked the scoop on the best party in town. By providing beer to minors, our parties automatically qualified as the best, because this was a product they could not easily provide themselves. During the week, the BFC scattered to all the local high schools to pass out flyers to our Friday- and Saturday-night parties:

Just $5 per person for all you can drink! Beer! Jell-O Shots! BFC Punch!

There wasn't a lot else to do in Conroe. Four or five hundred teenagers would show up in t-shirts and jeans, halter tops and cut-offs to drink all night long, sway to rock-and-roll, and puke till sunrise.

TABC tried to raid us more than once. That's the Texas Alcoholic Beverage Commission. We were ready for them. We picked sites that were hard for them to get to without us spotting them first, we loaded all the beer and booze and Jell-O shots in a single trailer, and we gave walkie-talkies to our small security team. The moment one of our security guys saw any telltale sign of the TABC's patrol vehicles, we'd lock the trailer and announce over a bullhorn, "TABC's here!" It was like kicking an ant bed. All the teenagers would scatter, including us. We locked the trailer and ditched it. We had already collected our money. They couldn't get into the trailer without breaking in, and what was the point when they had no suspects?

We threw three or four parties a year, and the raids were great for sales: further proof that these were bad-ass parties and the coolest game in town. As for the BFC, our four officers and loyal minions, we were more popular than the football team.

I might have been a Godless sinner, but I was also my father's son, an entrepreneur all the way, illegal or not. I set up a checking account for the BFC, and we put all our profits in there to split between us at the end of the year. We had very little overhead, mainly the booze and the band. We raked in several hundred dollars per party, so at year's end, the handful of committee members walked away with nearly a thousand bucks each. Not bad for slackers who didn't do much else.

At the end of my junior year, Mr. Green, my exasperated counselor, sent me to summer school. I usually showed up hung over after partying all night. But I passed.

***

I thought I wanted everything easy in high school, including the girls: easy on the eyes, easy to please, easy to switch from "no" to "yes." But senior year I fell for one who seemed high maintenance to me. Stephanie was a big personality, a popular girl, and a beauty. She was also a goody two-shoes. Although I ran with the BFC crowd, I was friends with everybody or I never would have met her. She hung out with athletes and brains, but I guess I was her bad-boy phase. She tried to reform me, like my counselor, like my sister Leslie, like my mom would have if she were alive— though if she were alive I probably wouldn't have needed so much reforming.

I let Steph believe her love would fix me. We talked about

marriage. Not like we were looking for banquet halls, but we agreed a wedding during her fourth year of college would be good. Of course, I never considered college. Even if I had not blown off school, I never had the money, hunger, or ability for that. I pictured goofing off until it was time to settle down. Then I'd get a good job, marry Steph, and have a bunch of kids.

That's not what happened.

Instead, Steph and I went to a house party, I got drunk outside, and she wandered inside. It started to rain, which drove the rest of us inside, which was when I noticed she was nowhere in sight. I walked upstairs to find her, with a sinking feeling I wasn't going to like what I found. I found my way to an empty bedroom, and opened the closet to find her inside with one of my buddies, Coby. It all seemed obvious now: how could she go through a bad-boy phase without becoming a bad girl? What really felt inevitable was that anyone I loved seemed sure to abandon me, one way or another.

I knew it was over. But I was all, "Let's go, Coby! Come on, we're gonna throw down!"

"Don't do this, Keith!" Steph said. "It's not Coby's fault. You and me have been over for a while."

By that I understood she and Coby had been fooling around for a while. But this wasn't about Steph anymore. It was about me and my rage. Coby was an offensive lineman, pure muscle. I was a has-been cross-country runner, my muscle all gone to beer. But he had broken the buddy code, and he owed me a punch. So, he followed me out front, surely knowing he would win in the end.

Driving rain poured in my eyes as I screamed, "Hey, let's go! Let's go!"

Another football buddy of mine, Clay, stepped between us.

"Keith, you don't wanna do this. You don't wanna go there. Break it up."

"Man, you get away from me!" I shoved Clay as hard as I could.

"You do that again, you're gonna get hurt," he said.

"Oh, you want some of this?" I pushed Clay again. I'd all but forgotten Coby, the guy I'd challenged to this fight.

Next thing I knew, Clay slugged me in the eye, I hit the ground, and he was on top of me. My head was in the mud, and he kept punching me in my face as rain dripped from his. A couple of guys pulled him off. That's when I realized it wasn't just rain spilling from Clay. He was crying. We'd been friends since grade school. His mom was my sixth-grade teacher.

"I'm sorry, man," he said.

By the end of the party, my eye was sealed shut, and Clay's hand was a bloody hunk of meat. We spent the rest of the night laughing at how Coby got the girl, while I got a ruined face and Clay got a busted-up hand.

Steph dated Coby for a while, but they didn't get married either. I wasn't all that broken up about it. Stephanie and I were bound to split up anyway. She was college bound, and I was anything but. I went on to date more girls, drink more beer, and ditch more than half my final semester of high school.

***

One Monday morning I got brought down to the dean's office. Miss Rutherford was a gray-haired grandma full of sweet but tough Old Texas charm. She called me to her office more than most students. I was sure this visit was about ditching classes.

"Mr. Isbell, come here and sit down," she always beckoned me, like she was about to offer me cookies. I was sure she liked me, sure I had her fooled into thinking I was a sweet Christian boy. Looking back, I think I underestimated her. Sure, I might have charmed her, but I doubt I fooled her. It was more like she thought I was interesting. I seem to recall she once said something like that: "You're an interesting case, Keith. I see something in you. Potential. You can do so much. Why are you wasting your talents on parties every night? Oh, yes, I know what you kids do." I hated the way adults acted like having fun made teenagers ridiculous, like they had already had all the fun and squeezed everything out of it and found it pointless.

This time, though, I was surprised to find two police officers standing inside Dean Rutherford's office, waiting for me. There was only one reason they could be there. The BFC had thrown another party Saturday night. The TABC and the cops had descended, and we'd scattered again. Miss Rutherford asked me to sit, but left the two officers standing behind me. I suspected they did this to frighten me, but at 17 I thought it was kind of exciting, an outlaw movie where I was the star.

"Normally you've got to deal with me, Keith," Dean Rutherford said, "but now you're going to have to deal with these gentlemen."

I turned to them with a grin. I wasn't putting on a poker face. I wasn't sweating bullets. I was enjoying this. More notoriety for the BFC could only be good for our rep, and that was good for business. "Okay, what do you need, officers?"

One of them said, "Keith, we know you're running an illegal business."

"Okay, officer," I said. "So, what're we here to do?"

The other one said, "We're not after you. We want to know who's buying the beer."

"I'm not going tell you that," I said.

"Well, if you don't tell us, we can arrest you for selling alcohol to minors."

"Who says I'm selling anything to anybody?"

Miss Rutherford shook her head at me, a warning I was taking this too far.

I appreciated her trying to help, but taking things too far was what I was all about. "Look, y'all need to do whatever you're gonna do to me, but I'm not telling you where I get my beer."

"We know it's not just you. We know you have co-conspirators."

I seem to recall Miss Rutherford jumping in at that moment, suggesting their language was too much like something you'd say to a murderous Mafioso and not to a 17-year-old high school senior. But after she took them down a peg, she still turned to me and said, "Keith, you need to tell them where the beer's coming from because they think they know. If you don't help them, they're going to catch the culprit anyway, but then they could put you in jail too—even if you are a minor. This is a serious crime." She gave me a pleading look that told me she really was trying to throw me a lifeline.

I didn't want it. Mafioso or high school senior, I was no snitch. "Look, I'm sorry, but I'm not going to do that."

We went in circles for a while until Miss Rutherford suggested they just let me go back to class, and they did. I think one of them warned me, "This isn't over." I figured that was just something losers say when it's over.

The BFC were winners. We were athletes. Okay, some of us were *former* athletes. But we were lords of the school. We even had the yearbook staff take a photo of our small crew and paid to put The BFC in the ad section like a legit business. If the cops were serious about finding my co-conspirators, they could have just flipped through the yearbook!

Several months later, the police raided my brother's apartment. They found a flyer for a BFC party going on that night, right at that moment. The invite was sitting on his table, out in the open for anyone to see. Kyle confessed to buying our beer, half a dozen kegs or more at a pop. I think he was trying to protect me, though he didn't have to. By the time the cops hit our party, we had booked out of there, once again leaving only the trailer, scattered red Solo cups, and the smell of spilled beer behind.

Kyle spent two or three days in jail. Our dad bailed him out. The judge gave him probation and community service.

As for me, I failed English the first semester of senior year. Not Miss Cook's class, someone else's. My counselor, Mr. Green, let me take a special test, said, "If you pass this test, we'll pass you for your last semester of English." I took the test. Mr. Green never told me the results, just told me I passed. Sometimes I suspect he lied about that, though I like to believe it was a white lie and maybe I came close to passing. I think part of him wanted me gone, while another part of him didn't want to let this 17-year-old punk trash his whole life because his mother died.

Mr. Green probably had more faith in my future than my dad did at that point. I suspect Dad looked at most of us kids and saw no future at all, just a family in ruins.

My big sister was the only one who seemed determined to escape what felt like a family curse. Leslie graduated in the top ten percent of her class, won multiple scholarships, and went away to Sam Houston State University. After that, there was nobody left at home to try to hold the rest of us together. Not that we had listened to her anyway. Much as she looked and acted like our mom, nobody could replace our mom. The rest of us continued our downhill slide: Kyle had a criminal record, I was the Kegger King of Conroe, and Julie chased the night like her brothers. We all knew she was running around with some guy or other, we just didn't know who.

**

Grad night, I took my teen degeneracy to the next level. My friends and I celebrated at a teen nightclub where they don't serve alcohol. No problem: I planned to try ecstasy for the first time. A friend of mine bought the X, and I paid him $20 a tablet. I loved the first hit, instantly felt why it's called the love drug. The room pulsed with music, lights, and dancing bodies. The girls caressed each other like they couldn't help themselves, the guys gave each other the kind of hugs usually reserved for big football wins, and the couples who paired up—they disappeared from view fast. I loved every last person there like we were one big family, like life was infinite, like even if there was no God we were all connected and it was beautiful.

I wanted to feel more of that, so less than an hour later I took a second tablet. Two was too much. I might have taken another after that, I don't remember. I only remember I wigged out, balled up in a corner, eyes rolled back, teeth grinding. Full of so much love and positive energy I could not move. Still I wanted more of this feeling. More love, love, love, love.

During a brief lucid moment that night or next morning, I decided I was tired of listening to my dad beg me to stop wasting my life, probably because I knew I was. I figured it was mine to waste if I wanted. I asked one of my buddies from the BFC crew, Daryll,

"Can I crash on your couch?" Daryll and I had been buddies since freshman year. Before he became a pothead, he used to work for my dad.

Next day I moved in with Daryll and his parents. I'm not sure he asked their permission. His mom and dad didn't look thrilled to see me, although his mom fed me dinner that first night, said it looked like it had been a long time since I'd eaten a good home-cooked meal.

That made me feel guilty. I thought about Leslie, who was a pretty good cook, thought about our mom who taught her, thought about all the dinners I'd skipped since she'd died, trying to avoid a night like this, sitting around the table with family. After the first night at my buddy's house, eating his mom's comfort-food casserole, I avoided sitting at their dinner table again. Usually I went out and grabbed a burger somewhere.

CHAPTER FIVE

THE DRAWER

For a good tree does not bear bad fruit, nor does a bad tree bear good fruit. For every tree is known by its own fruit. For men do not gather figs from thorns, nor do they gather grapes from a bramble bush. – Luke 6:43 - 44

Anything that made me feel good, my favorite amount of it was always "more." I loved ecstasy, better known as X, so I continued to take two to three times the normal dose even though that typically left me drooling in a corner. Then a friend gave me acid and suggested I combine it with X. Together, he called it "ax." What a combo! Acid made me hallucinate, which was cool, but taken alone it could leave me with Jell-O-brain. Coupling acid with ecstasy doubled the pleasure without the pitfalls: ecstasy made my acid dreams more awake, while acid made the whole ecstasy love-fest more ecstatic. On ax, I couldn't stop laughing. I failed to imagine what could be wrong with living a life this hilarious. And there was no longer anyone around to tell me otherwise.

Daryll's parents were the sweetest people I'd ever known besides my parents, but they had no rules. Which was why I moved in with them. Daryll's parents put me up in his sister's old room when it became clear I wasn't leaving anytime soon. His dad was a cop, but that didn't scare me. He was rarely around at night. His mom wasn't one of those moms who try to be cool by buying beer for her teenager's punk friends. She was just oblivious, the kind of woman who assumes if she behaves like a good person her children will follow, no other input required. I had a free roof overhead and freedom to be as bad as I wanted to be. I invited girls to stay the night in my room, sometimes a different girl each week. We did drugs anywhere in the house where we could close a door: Daryll, our buddies, our girlfriends, and me.

The drugs started as a casual pastime, just another way to party. School was over, it was summer, and I had no college plans. I was 18, and future and responsibility were far away. After spending the previous summer in summer school, I decided I deserved this vacation. So, I went to nightclubs, and drank or did drugs every night of the week. There was nothing anybody would put in front of me I wouldn't try, unless it involved a needle—I was afraid of those, and I thought so long as I avoided them it meant I wasn't an addict. My buddies and I kept our vices simple: drank beer, listened to loud music, cruised, picked up girls.

We were just killing time. But time refused to die.

If X and acid were exciting, then cocaine was a no-brainer. If coke was a rocket-to-the-moon, then crack was the low-budget, bottle-rocket version, perfect for a minimum-wage worker with no prospects. From there, I tested goofy stuff that made no sense. I took niacin, five or six at a time, for the sudden flush of heat. Some doofus told me I could get high smoking a cigarette coated in toothpaste, so I tried that too. My lungs smelled minty fresh, but it hurt like hell. Was that the high? I felt like a loser, but that didn't stop me: "Whoo! Let me try some more of that toothpaste!" Anything to change the way I felt for a few minutes, hours, or days.

Anything besides normal life, anything that made me forget who I was, where I was going, what I was doing. Or why.

About two dozen of my friends and I wandered like nomads from apartment to apartment, house to house, party to party. "What're we doing tonight?" someone would ask. "We're all meeting at Joe's," or "We're all meeting at Daryll's." Joe and Daryll and a few of the others were small-time drug dealers. The rest of us had nothing better going on in our lives. Before we came down from that night's drunk or high or both, the question would make the rounds again, "What're we doing tomorrow night?"

I earned enough money to stay high, though not much more than that, by taking odd jobs. One buddy had a lawn business, so I cut grass for him. He paid cash. I did a brief stint as a grocery sacker. A few months later, I got fired from that job when I called in sick from a skanky hotel room in Galveston after an all-night bender with a girl I met at the beach. I never did get her name.

Over the next couple of years, I moved into a series of apartments with a series of roommates and worked a series of restaurant jobs. I managed to get promoted from dishwasher to busboy to cook to waiter, but I got fired from almost all of them. If I didn't get fired, I quit. I screwed up every job because that's who I was: a screw-up. I didn't care. I kind of liked the rep.

My little sister, Julie, introduced me to a guy who managed a local restaurant where she liked to eat in Conroe. He was 32 when she was 17, and I didn't like the way he eyeballed her, so I decided off the bat he was a jerk. She convinced me to ask him for a job waiting tables there, and the way she flirted with him I knew he only offered me the position because of her. But I needed money for rent, food, beer, and drugs, so I convinced myself I could put up with him, even though I never put up with anything from anybody.

To my drug-warped mind, that restaurant manager was an authoritarian ass. In reality, he was probably just humorless, insensitive, and low on understanding. A robot kind of guy. I just didn't like him. No matter what he asked me to do, even if it was in my job description, his tone made it sound unreasonable. One night I was working a busy shift and didn't have time for a break, but I was hungry so I ordered fried mozzarella sticks to eat on the run. Likely the sight of me reaching for snacks in the middle of a rush is what gave him the itch to target me for his next demand. He told me to pick up two extra tables that weren't in my station.

"Can't do it. I'm swamped." I popped a mozzarella stick in my mouth.

"You don't look swamped."

"What? This?" I chewed in his face. "I haven't had a break all night, I haven't made one complaint about that, and I've done everything you've thrown at me. But I'm starving. That doesn't mean I have time for another table."

"Look, I'm not asking, I'm telling you: I need you to get out there and take those tables."

"You know what? I've been listening to you and listening to you, and you never listen to me. I'm sick of it." I took off my apron and threw it on the ground. Then I grabbed my little metal basket of mozzarella sticks and started to walk out.

He chased after me. "That basket doesn't belong to you!"

I stopped to face him. "You want this? Fine!" I took each mozzarella stick out of the basket one by one and threw them at him, pelting him with a couple before he could dodge them. Then I dropped the basket on the floor and walked out.

My next stop was waiting tables at a chain restaurant where the bartender was a partier who shared my new anti-work ethic. She liked to do shots with me and other aspiring young partiers on the food-serving staff—while we were on the clock. Those were the nights I was most lucid. Other nights, I was too wasted on drugs to show up at all.

At Christmas, I was supposed to play Santa Claus for the customers, but I was so strung out I called in sick. I had lost count of how many times I'd already done that. The next time I came in, the manager, Ron, pulled me into his office, and I knew I was fired. What surprised me was the way he did it: he didn't shout, get mad, or act self-righteous. He gave me the look my mom used to give me when I misbehaved, not disappointed so much as concerned.

"You're going down the wrong path, Keith," he said, "and you've got to get this right while there's still time. I'm going to share something with you, because I want you to know that I get it: I used to do drugs. I've been in your shoes, and I know it doesn't lead anywhere good. But if you get it together, if you turn this corner, you can still make something of yourself."

It was hard to look at him, hard to bear that sort of kindness when I didn't deserve it. "But if I make something of myself I'll have to do it somewhere else, because I'm fired, right?"

"That's right, Keith, but I'll still be rooting for you. And if you ever need someone to talk to, my door's open."

Ron held out his hand, so what could I do but shake it?

Plenty of people reached out like that. Plenty of them had been friends with my mom, and I figured they felt sorry for me. I never asked myself, "What's so wrong with that?"

***

Not long after that kinder, gentler firing, my father called. "Come over to the house, Keith." It was not a request, and the dutiful son that still lurked under my snarky demeanor didn't question him.

I still saw Dad from time to time. No doubt when he saw me he saw what everyone saw. If "every tree is known by its own fruit," then I bore the fruit of an addict: skin and bones, pale, dark circles under my eyes, clothes that looked slept in, the lost look of the unemployable. Kyle and Leslie were in touch with both Dad and me, and they surely filled in the blanks for him.

It was a hot, sunny day when I arrived at the house to find my dad on the roof. He was wearing shorts but no shirt, lying on a beach towel, smothered in some kind of oil.

"Hey, Dad!" I hollered. "What're you doing up there?

"Tanning. What does it look like I'm doing?"

"What on earth for?"

"Would you just get up here, son?"

"Can't you come down here?"

"Why? Too hung over to manage a ladder?"

No safe way to answer that, so, with a roll of my eyes, I climbed the ladder. I never did find out what was up with the tanning. Maybe he wanted to look young and fit to impress his employers or clients at the insurance company. Maybe he'd started dating again. I had no idea what was going on in his life, too wrapped up in my own life to care. I knew my life was in the toilet and it was my fault, and this made me feel so sorry for myself I could not bear to look at him. His opinion still mattered to me, but not enough to convince me to make any kind of effort.

He said more or less what my last restaurant manager had said, "I gotta tell ya, your life is just a mess, Keith. I think you're absolutely going down the wrong path. I know your mom would be disappointed."

"I know, Dad, I know. I'll do better at the next job."

"That's what you always say. I think you need some support, son, because you're just not getting there on your own. There's no shame in needing a little help. We all do now and then. So, here's what I propose: I'm willing to take you back into this house, but you've got to follow my rules. I'll get you some work, so you'll have a paycheck." He offered to charge me no more than a pittance for rent, "until you get back on your feet."

"That's really generous, Dad. I appreciate it. I'll let you know."

I never went back.

***

I did take my father up on his offer to help me find work. He put in a good word with a friend of his who worked for the city, who gave me a job as a meter reader for the water department. That job blew: dogs chased me, and sometimes so did people when I came to cut off their water. I brought my little cocaine spoon with me to work, so I could snort on the job. Getting hold of blow was easier than ever thanks to my new roommate, Jason, a guy who knew all the right connections.

Even though I didn't move home, Dad invited me to come over on my birthday for an afternoon party with extended family: my brother and sisters, cousins, aunts, uncles, and Maw Maw. That's what we all called our grandma, my mom's mom. "I'll buy a cake," Dad said.

I forgot about that party. Jason and I stayed up the night before at our apartment, doing our own brand of partying with Daryll, several other friends, and girls, girls, girls. My buddies toasted my birthday all night long with beer and lines of coke, but then, that was how we spent most nights. Next day a bunch of us guys were still passed out all over Jason's apartment, when I heard a distant pounding and shouting.

The front door crashed open and next thing I knew Kyle was standing over me where I lay on the floor. "You gotta get up right now! You're coming with me!"

I squinted at him. The light from the open door hurt. I think the sun was setting. I'd missed most of the day. "What for?"

"Dad's having a birthday party for you, remember?"

"Oh, right. I forgot."

"Come on, let's get you dressed."

"What? No. Are you kidding? I can't go anywhere. I'm too hung over."

"Listen to me, Keith: you are going to do this. We got family there, and the only person that hasn't shown up is you. You need to come right now."

"No way!" I was not about to walk into my own birthday party two hours late and looking like hell. I think I convinced him to leave by asking, "You really want Maw Maw to see me like this?"

***

Jason, my roommate and cocaine connection, was also a college student, one of the best in his class. One day, he left for school before I went to work, and like most days, he did a line of coke before he left the apartment. I knew this because every morning I opened this particular bathroom drawer and saw traces of powder outlining where his line used to be, and parallel to that a neat little line of un-snorted coke he left just for me. One for him, one for me, because we were roomies, and let's face it, because we were codependent and it was in his interest to keep me hooked just like him.

For the first time, instead of snorting that line like I always did, I stared at it, like it might have something to tell me. That's when it struck me: Jason and I were two coke-heads with our own little sharing ritual. The longer I stared at that little white line, the more it looked like an arrow pointing to hell.

It was not nighttime. It was not party o'clock. It was breakfast-time, and I hadn't slept yet, showered yet, eaten yet. There was no cereal or milk in the house. This was not because I was broke—although that happened sometimes because most of my money went to drugs—but because neither Jason nor I had remembered to go to the store. Sometimes we forgot about food.

At that moment, I was not hungry for breakfast. All I was hungry for was this line of blow. Realizing that, I hesitated. In that moment, an inner voice said something I'd never considered before: "Okay, maybe there is no God controlling this world, but Keith, *you* definitely are not in control." This little line in the morning just to get my day started, it was dictating my life, making my decisions, robbing me of sleep for days at a time, eating my body away until I barely recognized myself in the mirror. "If you don't stop," the inner voice said, "this may be the last thing you ever see. Not today, but soon."

I walked away from the little white line, picked up the phone, and dialed the first number that came to mind. "Dad, I've got a problem."

"Are you in jail again?"

"No, it's cocaine."

We talked a while, and he said a bunch of stuff I'd heard a

million times: that admitting I had a problem was the first step, that addiction was an illness, that I had to give it up to God. "I know this great youth pastor who works with young guys who are trying to get off drugs."

"Dad, I'm not going to church."

"You don't have to go to church. I'm just asking you to talk to this guy. You know, he's not some old guy like me. He's young like you. I think you'll like him."

"Okay. Thanks, Dad." I'd already dismissed half of what he said, but I hung on to the only part of it that mattered to me then: my father still loved me, still hoped for me, still rooted for me. I was crying a little, not sure if I was feeling sentimental or just shaky with the need for my morning fix.

I hung up, closed the drawer, and quit doing coke right then, that morning in the bathroom. Then, because I told Dad I would, I went to the youth pastor and talked to him. Once. I never went back, but I stayed off the coke. Just made up my mind.

To avoid temptation, I moved out of Jason's apartment. Over the years to come, I heard stories of Jason and his battles with addiction. Ultimately, he managed to get through the drug-induced haze of college, get his degree, sober up, and make something of himself.

Shortly after I quit coke, Dad decided he needed a change too. He quit selling insurance and went to work for a Christian publishing company. His new employers were based right outside Chicago, and they asked him to move there. If there was a going-away party, I didn't make that one either. My attitude was, I don't live at home anyway, what does it matter where my father lives? My little sister had graduated high school but still lived at home, and she moved to Chicago with him. Dad didn't ask me to come, and I didn't mind. We both knew what my answer would be.

I still hung out with Daryll, even though he drank a lot of beer, sold a lot of pot, and dealt a little ecstasy now and then. I wasn't about to stop hanging with Daryll, because he was my best friend, my right-hand man. Anyway, beer and X weren't my problem, so I didn't quit those. And I still liked the occasional hit of acid. Sometimes I even toked a joint if it came my way, though I still hated it. But I tried to stick to weekend partying. It seemed a simple rule to maintain so long as I steered clear of cocaine. Because coke was my only problem. I had everything else under control.

CHAPTER SIX

THE CELL

"My guilt has overwhelmed me like a burden too heavy to bear."
– Psalms 38:4

Daryll helped distribute pot for a small-time operation run by an-other of our friends, who went by the nickname Sticks. Sticks was nuts. I wouldn't say he was mentally ill, but his behavior did reveal what some might call psychotic tendencies. I'll still say this for Sticks, though: he was loyal to his friends. If someone crossed any of us, he considered that the same as crossing him. And crossing Sticks could be bad for a person's health.

One evening, Sticks, another buddy named Kevin, and I all woke up at Daryll's after sleeping off an all-nighter. Sticks jumped up from the couch like he'd just been jolted by an electric shock and said, "We gotta go collect money from this guy that owes Daryll." I knew what this meant: Daryll owed Sticks money, but Sticks didn't want to threaten Daryll, because Daryll was his buddy. He needed to find the next guy down the supply chain to threaten, one of Daryll's buyers.

The four of us—Sticks, Daryll, Kevin, and I—hopped into Sticks' car, some sort of convertible, but not shiny and new, beat up and dented, the kind of car that looks like it enjoys long nights of bad company and good drugs. By the time we arrived at our destination, an apartment complex, my blood was pumping hot and fast, because "We gotta go collect money" typically meant "We gotta go start a fight." I was young and broke, and a good fistfight was about my only entertainment besides beer, recreational drugs, and TV.

Sticks sprang out of his car and made straight for a few guys standing in the parking lot drinking beers, so I figured either, a) one of them was the guy he was looking for, or b) these were friends of the guy he was looking for. I knew one of them, a guy named Danny. He was the kid brother of our friend, Randall. Randall was the guy whose house I'd been sleeping at, hung over as hell, the day my brother tried to drag me home to my own birthday party.

Sticks' usual modus operandi in a situation like this was to act like all he wanted was a friendly conversation, because they knew why he was really there, so he knew the buddy-buddy act would unnerve them, give them time to sweat. The longer he waited to bring up the money they owed, the more scared they'd be by the time he demanded payment or else.

That's not what he did this time. This time, he pulled a gun out of the waist of his jeans, grabbed Danny, shoved the gun into his mouth, and used it like a handle to pump him down to the ground. With Danny on his knees, Sticks said, "You're gonna pay Daryll back because Daryll owes me money. And if you don't pay Daryll, then Daryll can't pay me, can he?"

Of course, Danny couldn't reply right away because he had a gun in his mouth, and all I heard was teeth clacking on metal. I might have also heard a couple of Danny's friends mutter things, like, "Holy shit, man!" and "Who the hell's that?" and maybe some feet running down the parking lot and into the apartment building.

But I was fixated on the gun. "Whoa, dude! What're you doing?"

Sticks ignored me and kept demanding money from Danny. It occurred to me he might be on some sort of speed and maybe I'd best shut up. Then he acted like he had just woken up to the idea that his gun was preventing Danny from responding. "Oh, is this a problem, man?" He pulled the gun out of Danny's mouth but kept it pointed at him.

Danny started rapid-fire explaining how he didn't have Daryll's money on him right that minute. I wanted to shout, *Hey, Danny's our friend*, but it seemed unwise to contradict Sticks right then, what with the gun and all.

It wasn't like I'd never seen Sticks with a gun before. Or Daryll or Kevin for that matter. My friends always packed: guns stuffed in their pants, their pockets, the glove box. We were all Texans, and they were all drug dealers. I expected no less, although the only gun I owned was a 410 single-shot shotgun, which I only used for squirrel hunting.

Dad had raised my brother, sisters, and me with guns and taught us to respect them, to appreciate their usefulness for hunting and the possibility of defending home, life, and liberty. He also taught us to maintain a healthy fear of a gun's power to kill. I assumed my friends had been taught the same. Most drug deals that went bad they handled with fistfights. The guns had always been for show.

But Sticks was the wild card, and he liked that people saw him that way. For him a show of firepower wasn't enough: what did it mean unless he was willing to use it? Even though I was a little scared of him, I'll admit the adrenaline I felt at that moment was its own kind of high.

Somewhere in the midst of this confrontation, Randall's wife, also a friend of ours, ran out of her apartment, saw her brother-in-law on his knees in the bushes with four friends standing over him, and said what I had failed to say: "What's wrong with you? What kind of friends are you?"

Sticks put away the gun, but it had already done the trick. Danny asked for more time to pay, but Sticks said, "Daryll can't wait. Can you, Daryll?"

"Okay, okay," Danny said. "I know this guy who wants to buy my car."

We spent the rest of the night following Danny around while he made phone calls, drove to this guy's house, sold the guy his old beater car, and then paid Daryll the several hundred dollars he owed. Sticks stood by and watched, all magnanimous, like he was glad to see Daryll get justice.

Back at Daryll's place, Daryll counted most of those bills out into Sticks' hands.

Sticks said, "Thanks, buddy," all casual, like it was any another weekend night. Then he held the wad up. "Gentlemen, drinks are on me."

We all went to a nightclub to get wasted on the proceeds from the sale of Danny's car. I didn't approve of Sticks' method, but it was hard to argue with the result, so I let him buy me a few beers.

***

Sticks enjoyed his rep as a wild man, and didn't seem to care that some people hated him. Sometimes he used his convertible to chase down deadbeat buyers and run them off the road. These were quiet back roads without a lot of traffic, but I knew we could only test fate so many times, that someone might get killed, including us. I wondered what might happen if someone decided to turn the tables, to come after him for revenge. What if I was with him when that happened? I never sold drugs, so I never knew the whole flow-chart of relationships that made up his world, never knew for sure just how big a risk this friendship was.

Still, we didn't have to wait for any of his car chases to go bad for us to face off with death. One night I sat in a car with Sticks, and he wasn't trying to run anybody off the road, but he was drunk or high, and he simply lost control of his car, overcorrected, bounced into a ditch, and broke the tire clean off. We landed on top of the tire, otherwise the car would have flipped. I think the roof was down, so we would have been dead if not for that tire.

We stumbled out of the car and laughed our fool heads off. Hooted and hollered and jumped up and down.

"Whoa! That felt like flying!"

"I can't believe we're still alive!"

We walked to a payphone and called a friend to come get us. He had the car towed to a shop, and a few days later we were on the road again, Sticks driving drunk or high. To me this all seemed normal. Though by then I had left normal far in the rearview mirror.

Not long after, my best buddy, Daryll, got busted with two blocks of marijuana. I thought that was maybe twenty pounds, though I was no expert. I only knew it was a lot of dope. Maybe Daryll rolled over on Sticks, maybe not, but Sticks was later sentenced to ten years.

I knew it was only a matter of time before I died or landed in prison. But that future seemed fuzzy and far away, like everything when you're drunk.

***

I wasn't with Sticks or Daryll when it happened. I was with Marty, who said, "Hey, let's go wahoo some beer." Marty was one of my least out-of-control friends, though we were all a little reckless, and I didn't think wahooing beer was a big deal. Whenever we didn't have money for beer, which was often, we would just wahoo it, which means we'd run into the liquor store, grab a six-pack or two, run out, dive into the car, and tear out of there. Since it was only a couple of six-packs, typically the manager couldn't be bothered to call police, too much wasted time to recover a few bucks. The only time we drank anything as fine as a Miller Light or Budweiser was when we stole it. The rest of the time, we drank Schlitz, Black Label, or some cheapo three-dollar-a-twelve-pack beer that tasted like backwash.

We called the act of stealing beer "wahoo," because of the supposed hollering we did as we sped off: "Wahooooo!" Though I don't think we ever made that sound, just laughed like hyenas. Mostly, I guess we called it wahooing because we didn't want to think of ourselves as thieves. Who wanted to think about what it meant to be such lowlifes we felt compelled to steal six-packs?

For me, the key to wahooing beer was to stroll in like I knew what I wanted, grab two six-packs with confidence, not hide them, but swing them as I approached the register as if I had every intention of paying, then take a sharp turn at the last minute and run for it.

I started the routine like I had a hundred times: grabbed two six-packs of Bud, walked toward the front, tore on out the door, jumped in back of the car, and shouted, "Let's go!"

I never noticed the cop standing right in the aisle of the liquor store watching my every move, from the moment I walked in until I jumped in the car. Not a minute later, we heard the sirens and saw the flashing red lights. I could tell the cops were annoyed they had to waste time on such a penny-ante crime, and were eager to get this over with, just write us a ticket and let us go. But they ran my license and found a warrant for my arrest, not for drugs or stealing, but for a traffic ticket for speeding and reckless driving. That time, I had been driving maybe twenty miles over the speed limit when I cut into a parking lot, brakes squealing. That had happened months earlier, and I just blew it off, like everything else in my life.

"Looks like it's no warning for you this time. I'm taking you in," the officer said. "And I'm going to have to arrest your buddy too." He charged us both with theft.

***

It wasn't my first time in jail. I'd been thrown in a cell once before for driving without a license, across the state line in Louisiana. But that time, I'd sat on a bench waiting for a couple of hours for my dad to come get me, and the charges were reduced to a small fine. This time they threw Marty and me in a holding tank with some older drunks. For once I wasn't drunk, but these guys were throwing up, talking to themselves, and I think one guy was crying.

One of the drunks tried to pick a fight with me. "What're you looking at?"

"Nothin'."

"You sayin' I'm nothin'?"

"Look, you just leave me alone and I'll leave you alone."

"Don't tell me what to do!" Push.

"Don't touch me!" Shove.

That sort of thing.

A guard came in, broke us apart, and put me in a far cell by myself, not another soul in sight. I was surrounded by nothing but four walls, a heavy door, and one window too small and murky to see out of. There was a hard metal bench to sleep on. I felt too antsy to sleep anyway. I paced, unable to rest my eyes on anything to distract me: the walls were blank, but my mind was full of images I couldn't stop.

Normally at this time of night I was out partying, or working to make just enough money to keep partying, or sleeping. Now I was awake, and every emotion I had ignored since my mother's death ganged up on me. I heard my mother inside my head, asking: *How did you get here?* It wasn't like the answer was a mystery. Another voice in my head had long been telling me I was on a road that led to one of two destinations: prison or death. *But really, haven't you already been in prison, this whole time?* my mom asked. Even in death, Mom still had me pegged.

For the past four years, anytime I'd done anything I knew was wrong, I'd always thought of her, her look of disappointment, her words of admonishment, her soft encouragement to do better because I was her "little preacher." It was never enough to make me stop. And some embarrassed, guilty part of me had blamed her for all of it. I knew she was what all this was about: the drugs, the booze, the petty crime, all to avoid missing her.

None of us kids ever had any grief counseling, never talked to our dad or each other about loss, never prayed to God to help us carry our sorrow. The only time I was able to talk to anyone about my memories of Mom, happy or sad, was when I was sloppy drunk. Then I was able to cry. When I was sober I had to pretend I had moved on.

Except I hadn't. None of us had. Not my brother, my sisters, or my dad.

I felt abandoned in that cell. It was fitting, I guess, because that's how I'd felt from the moment my dad started wailing over my mother's dead body, her spirit vanished from our home. Abandonment was always there under the surface, and now here it was on top of me, sitting on my chest, staring me in the eye in a room where they never turned out the lights.

I spent four hours alone in that cell. Felt like four years.

Marty's dad had already picked him up and taken him home. Me, the guards took into a room for delousing. "You can't wear any colors," they said, in case I was in a gang. "If you have white underwear, white socks, you're fine, but if there's any colors they have to go in this bag."

I stripped down to my white t-shirt, white socks, and a pair of white boxers with little kissy faces all over them. I was one of a half-dozen half-naked suspects waiting in the doorway to the shower room. The guard gave us all a once-over, and stopped in front of me.

"Did you not understand what I said?"

"Yeah, I understood what you said."

"Well, you got colors on those underwear?"

"I guess so."

"Then take 'em off!"

So, I took them off, now naked from the waist down. The door to the shower was wide open so anybody walking past could see me. I felt sure they did this to humiliate me. If so, it worked. Then we prisoners walked into the shower room and closed our eyes while the guards sprayed a powder all over us to kill lice, from head to toe. My head was enveloped in this cloud that smelled like chemicals and I wondered if breathing it would give me cancer. I almost laughed, a little hysterical, because wasn't that what I'd been afraid of all along? That I was going to die of cancer like my mom? Wasn't that why I was living like there was no tomorrow?

A guard handed me an orange jumpsuit and a mat, and sent me to the misdemeanor tank, with the other five guys. There was no place to lie down, so I spent the night lying on the cold floor. There was a toilet out in the open, and I put off going as long as I could, but sooner or later I had to take a crap.

The only things I remember that tank having were that toilet, an incomplete set of dominoes, and a TV tuned to cartoons 24/7. I didn't want to play dominoes or watch cartoons. The clack of the domino tiles and the circus music of the cartoons circled around my head, louder and louder, until I covered my ears. I could still hear the loud *Boom!* every time the door to the tank opened and closed. I would look up, hopeful someone had come to get me.

Nobody came.

A day went by, then two. Still nobody showed to bail me out. Not my brother, big sister, or friends, even though I knew they all knew where I was, even though I knew Marty had spread the word. I knew that when my dad left for Chicago he had asked my aunt to keep an eye on us three eldest kids, who had stayed behind in Conroe. She never showed either.

I broke down and asked to use one of the jailhouse phones to call my father. The moment he spoke, I knew he had told my aunt to let me fall.

"I'm not going to get you out this time," Dad said, his voice sounding smaller than the thousand miles between us could account for. "You earned your way in there. You just stay there for a while and think."

So that's what I did, even though I'd had enough of thinking. That's what I did, because there was nothing else to do.

Chapter Seven

The Actor

Then Peter came to Him and said, "Lord, how often shall my brother sin against me, and I forgive him? Up to seven times?" Jesus said to him, "I do not say to you, up to seven times, but up to seventy times seven." – Matthew 18:21-22

I returned to the holding tank to digest my father's words: "I'm not going to get you out this time." That was when I knew: I'm done in this town. I'm a 21-year-old drug addict, I'm unemployable, I'm running with the wrong people. If I keep partying with criminals, I'll end up sitting in a cell watching cartoons for the rest of my life.

The cartoons weren't funny anymore, not Road Runner, not Bugs Bunny, not Scooby Doo, because in real life if I kept chasing trouble until I fell off a cliff, that would be the end of me. I listened to the heavy metal door open and close: *Boom! Boom! Boom!* Every time it closed, I was still in there. I wanted out, and once I got out, I wanted to go as far away as possible. Not just far from the jail. Far from Conroe.

A few days later, my brother showed and bailed me out. I went back to Daryll's house, but only long enough to tell him I was leaving town.

He didn't look surprised, just kicked back on the couch like this was no biggie. "Me too. I'm moving to Austin to go to community college."

It sounded perfect. "Maybe I can go with you."

"Man, I wish I could hook you up, but it's me and three other guys. We're gonna get an apartment together. I don't know if there's a spot for you." His words stung, but not as much as I would have expected. Daryll had always been there for me in the past, but maybe that was one of the reasons I was stuck in a rut, spinning my wheels.

His mom called from the kitchen, "Keith, honey, you can stay here with us just as long as you want. As far as I'm concerned, you're family."

"That's so sweet of you," I said. "But no. I really need a change."

I was scared I had already waited too long, if even my most outlaw friends were already cleaning up their act and clearing out.

I took a risk and called my dad again. "Dad, please don't hang up. I'm not in jail anymore and I'm not asking you to bail me out, but I am begging you to help me get out of this town. I gotta get outta here because if I don't, I'm either gonna end up dead or in prison. I know I don't deserve another chance, but I'm ready to start over, and I just don't have anywhere else to go. Can I stay with you a while?"

He sounded like he had been holding his breath since I'd called from jail days before. "You better believe it. But you're going to play by my rules. You're going to do what I tell you, you're going to school, and we're going to figure out which direction you're going in your life. Anything short of you doing what I say and this isn't going to work." His words were firm but his tone was loving. I heard it not as an ultimatum, but an invitation to something I thought had vanished.

Family.

"Absolutely. Whatever you say, Dad. Really." A mere few weeks before I might have rolled my eyes at his demands. But at this point, I felt nothing but gratitude. I'd gone so far off the rails I wouldn't have been surprised if he had given up on me. But I think we both realized he'd gone off the rails too.

In my memory, Mom had been the glue that held our family together, but now I remembered it had been the two of them together. Dad had coached all my teams, had taught me the value of work, had hunted and fished with me, had prayed with me. Then Mom died, but he was the one who became a ghost. We became a family of ghosts. I could hear in his voice that he needed a second chance as much as I did, a chance to be a dad again.

My 19-year-old baby sister, Julie, had recently returned to Conroe. She had only stayed with Dad in Chicago a couple of months before she found out she was pregnant. Turned out she had been secretly dating the restaurant manager I hated, the one I had quit on during a rush, the one I'd pelted with deep-fried mozzarella sticks. If I had known that this creep, who was fifteen years older than Julie, had been fooling around with her, I would have decked him that day. She ended up marrying him. I felt bad for her, but it meant Dad had a spare room for me.

I didn't own a car, so my father flew to Texas to buy me one for the big move. Maybe if he'd known how few belongings I owned or how little car he could afford, he might have bought me a plane ticket. But we both accepted the idea that a cross-country move meant a road trip. So, he bought me a cramped Toyota Camry on its last legs. Then he bought me a map, marked my route in black marker, and flew back to Chicago to wait for my arrival.

It took me a week or so to leave, not because I had a lot to pack or a job to quit or a girlfriend to break up with. I just didn't know how to say goodbye to the only home I'd ever known and all the people in it, even the jackasses I thought I hated. Not that it was a tearjerker sort of farewell. I drank a lot of beer, because that's how they give a send-off in Conroe.

Then I threw a garbage bag full of my clothes in the back of the Camry, and with that I was packed. I drove for two days. Most of the trip was on freeways, where I had to hold the Camry's gearshift in fifth or it would pop out. The air conditioner broke down early on day one, and it was high summer, so I rolled down the windows. The FM radio didn't work, so all I could listen to was AM. So, with arm aching and skin sweating, I listened to newscasters, evangelists, and golden oldies all the way to Chicago.

Maybe Dad was right, about a road trip being a necessary ingredient to a cross-country move. Hours alone in a jail cell had hit me with the fear to quit my old life, but hours alone on the open road filled me with the hope to embrace a new one. I didn't waste much time looking in the rearview mirror. I was running away from my old idea of home, which was more about familiarity than anything. Now I would have to redefine home in an unfamiliar place among unfamiliar people, including my dad. But I was eager to reclaim the best of that relationship.

Heading north toward my father, I felt like I was once again following the true north of the moral compass my mom had tucked inside me. Dad had always been a good man, and hard work central to his goodness. He would tell me what to do, and if I just did it, then maybe I could be something of the man he once was. And maybe he could too.

***

The final few miles to Dad's that old Camry complained non-stop, squealing and sputtering. I pulled into his apartment complex right as the engine died. I managed to park the car, but it never moved again. It had served its purpose. Like it knew this was where I was supposed to be.

I dragged my garbage bag upstairs and knocked on Dad's door. He showed me around the apartment like he was showing off a brand new 5,000-square-foot model home. He had made the second bedroom up to look more like a guy's room, or maybe that was simply the result of him eliminating all signs of my sister, who had so disappointed us both that by unspoken agreement we barely mentioned her.

Then he and I went out for burgers, and he laid down the rules. I was ready for rules. Rules sounded good.

I had to be home by midnight every night. I had to get up every morning no later than 9:00, regardless of the day of the week or what I had scheduled for the day. I had to go to school, go to work, go to church. I had to share chores around the apartment, but then he'd always given me chores back when I'd lived at our home in Conroe.

None of it sounded unreasonable on its face, but I'd grown unused to accountability, and I knew I had my work cut out for me. This wasn't a homecoming. It was desperation. This might be my only chance to get my life together. In the first five minutes, I could tell Dad was never going to get his life all the way together. Some part of him would always be with my mother. He never had been a touchy-feely guy to begin with, but I felt a space between us neither of us could cross. Still, it felt good to talk again without the feeling we'd both rather be elsewhere.

Within a week I landed a job bartending for a little restaurant and bar in Elgin. My regulars were all local car salesmen who stopped by to drink before work, during work, after work. Since my car was dead and I had no money of my own yet, I took a cab to and from work. The cab rides were expensive, but my dad didn't charge me rent, so I could afford the extra expense and it gave me better control of my time. My dad's work ethic, which I determined to make my work ethic, called on me to never be late.

As for the free room, this wasn't my dad going soft on me. He just wanted me to become independent as soon as possible, and he knew I needed to save for my own car and apartment, which was sure to require first and last month's rent plus a deposit.

My dad did not know I was an atheist, that I believed God was a fairytale made up to comfort people who feared death. I went to church with him, kept my mouth shut about what I did and didn't believe, and hoped that wasn't the same as lying. Thanks to my new job, sometimes I could wiggle out of it: "Sorry, Dad, I can't make church today."

Although living with my father did not renew my faith in God, the change of scene did help me visualize myself as a new man capable of a new life. Maybe that new life surrounded me with bottles of booze and alcoholic car-salesmen, but it was a step up from lines of coke and gun-toting drug dealers. I did not love my job, but I held on to faith that if I kept showing up and doing what I needed to do, my purpose would reveal itself. I went to work, came home by midnight, and woke by nine to start all over again.

My father's rules helped me return to something like normal. Normal felt good, but not quite enough. So, I shaped dad's way into something that felt more like my way.

My dad had commanded me to go to college, but he had not specified what I had to study. In my mind, America had three major cities—New York, L.A., and Chicago—and these were places where people made their mark. I decided this meant I should be an actor. There was no reason for me to think that. I had never taken a drama class in my life, had never starred in a school play, had never given acting much thought at all. But God knew I was never shy. Women often told me I was handsome, my mother used to call me her little preacher, and I loved telling stories to anyone who would listen. Take any good preacher or good bartender: Didn't they all have charisma, stage presence, a flair for performance?

I went to the local community college and signed up for a class in method acting. I didn't sign up for a single other class.

My dad tried to be supportive. "If that's what you really want to do. You never know, Keith. It could happen." I saw the doubt in his eyes, but even if there was only a one percent chance of me making it as an actor, this was better than a ninety-nine percent chance of me winding up dead or in jail, the future I'd been chasing in Conroe.

On the first day of class, the teacher asked me to stand in front of everyone and pretend to be bacon in a frying pan, and then seaweed in the bottom of the ocean. I laughed my way through the entire exercise. I thought, *this is stupid.* I never went back to class.

That night, pouring drinks, I told my regulars, "What a bunch of baloney. I'm going to find some real acting classes." I went to a studio that offered classes in film acting. I lasted longer in that class: two days.

Then I met with an agent, and she flattered me that I had what it took to be a star. "You're a natural," she said. I took that to mean I was going to be the next Luke Perry, star of *Beverly Hills 90210*.

The agent said all I needed were headshots, or maybe that's all I heard her say. So, I spent hundreds of my hard-earned tips on a professional photographer for a photo shoot and a box of head-shots. I sent a stack to my agent and never saw her again. She called now and then, suggested I go to this or that audition, but I never went to any of them. "It was just some cheapo local commercial. It didn't seem worth missing a shift," I might tell the guys at the bar, or "It was a cattle call. Hundreds of guys lined up like hookers in a police lineup. Who needs the humiliation?"

I guess the idea of acting sounded easy, stepping onto a stage or in front of a camera and pretending to be somebody else. I'd been the life of the party for years, and everybody loved me in that role. Surely, I would be good at any role I took on. I figured if I put my mind to it, I could do it. But I had no passion for it. Trouble was, I didn't know if I had a passion for anything.

***

For six months or so I floated through my shifts at the bar like it was nothing more than a way station while I waited to land my big break as an actor. Instead, I landed a new job bartending at a high-end bar owned by one of the biggest big-shots in Chicago. I made good money and made friends with the other employees. Restaurant employees tend to be a young, single, partying kind of crowd, and I was eager to fit in.

Most of us worked late, then spent our tips in the bar, drinking well past last call, sometimes till four in the morning. We were young, the future was far away, and my life still held a million pos-sibilities. Laughing all night long did not seem out of line with either my dad's rules or my vague goal to make my mark. These guys were not like my friends back home, where drugs were an everyday ritual.

One night, one of the waiters whispered to me, "Hey Keith, I've got some cocaine. You wanna do some?"

I didn't hesitate. "Sure."

Why not? It wasn't like I was an addict. I'd never gone through withdrawals when I quit cocaine. So why would I say no to something I knew felt so good? This scene wasn't hardcore. We were just having fun. Just one line couldn't hurt. I followed him into the bathroom.

That one line shot through me like a religious experience. Accepting Jesus in my heart had never made me feel that kind of jolt. In that second I knew: "I can never go down this road again." That was it, I never did a single recreational drug again. I refused to screw up my second chance.

I still had an occasional drink after work. But the less I drank, the more fun I had, especially on the job. I was a flair bartender, flipping and juggling bottles and glasses to impress my customers, and making big tips doing it. I was happy to work a double just to help out a fellow employee. I loved hanging with the customers, the waiters and bartenders and cooks, the food and beverage vendors, even the managers. Having a good work ethic wasn't hard once I stopped doing drugs, because it became easier to remember how much I enjoyed people. And restaurants are all about people.

I even enjoyed being called on to deal with people in explosive situations. One night I was bartending when two booming male voices rose above the murmuring crowd. I looked up to see two young guys verbally sparring in front of the big stone fireplace at the end of the bar, bodies tense, faces inches from each other, spitting words like automatic gunfire. This was not some low-budget dive bar but a fine-dining establishment, and their behavior was out of sync with the big-price-point atmosphere.

The general manager, Ernie, a big Italian tough-guy with a Chicago accent like some Al Capone throwback, made his way to me. "Keith, can you go see what's going on with those guys?"

The words barely left his mouth before I headed toward the end of the bar closest to the stone fireplace. I'd been serving the two arguing men, so I adopted a casual tone, as if to suggest *We're all friends here.* "Hey, guys, knock it off."

Just as I said that, one guy slugged the other guy and sent him reeling into the stone fireplace. My approach to solving this problem was to take off running and prepare to launch myself over the top of the bar and throw myself at them like a pole-vaulter. Instead, I hooked my foot on the edge of the bar rail, and when I tried to push off the rail, it broke. So instead of clearing the bar, I slammed into the top of it and slid into two beer glasses, which just happened to belong to the two guys, and the glasses went flying off the end of the bar and broke. Some of the shards came with me as I crashed into the fighting pair and grabbed them on my way down. The three of us landed in a heap on the floor, and a huge shard of glass ripped one guy's arm wide open. Blood everywhere.

Police came. It was a mess. But afterward, Ernie did not criticize me. Just said something like, "You're good at talking to people. Maybe next time try going around the bar and, you know, talking."

I laughed. "Talking I can do."

In the days, weeks, months that followed, some of my coworkers said, "You love being here so much. Why don't you go into management?"

"No way. I make better money as a bartender. Anyway, I'm gonna be an actor."

Nobody laughed when I said that. My coworkers said I had such a gift of gab I could convince anybody of anything. I assumed that skill would be an asset for an actor. In the meantime, it didn't hurt me as a bartender. I flirted with female customers, which helped increase the size of my tips. I always told pretty women I was an actor, even though it had been months since I'd done anything other than type my agent's name on a resume and get my headshots.

"You're an actor? What have you done? Anything I might've seen?"

I was always honest. "Well, I really haven't done anything yet. But it's coming." I repeated this so many times I believed it.

I dated a customer or two, as well as women I met hanging out with friends. I had maybe a couple of serious girlfriends in a couple of years. But neither of them gave me the feeling that they could make my world, the kind of feeling I knew my dad had for my mom.

One afternoon when business was slow Ernie—the GM who looked like a Mafioso—pulled me aside. "You have a few minutes?"

"Sure, boss."

He led me to a table, where I sat across from him. "So, Keith, how's the acting thing going?"

"Well, you know, my agent keeps calling, but the right thing just hasn't come along yet."

He did that thing where you don't exactly roll your eyes but you sort of let someone see the potential for you to roll your eyes. "So, you're really not doing anything."

"Not right now, but I'm going to. I've got some great headshots, and my agent thinks they're going to get me some good gigs. Would you like to see 'em?"

"No thanks. Look, I'm going to be honest with you, Keith, I don't really think acting is what you're here to do."

"At this restaurant?"

"In this life. Let me tell you what I think: I think it works with the girls, but other than that I think you're wasting your time with all this. You're not an actor, and you're never really going to be. That said, there's nothing you can't do in this restaurant."

"Yeah, that's true," I said. "I can do it all."

"I see in you real talent. Have you ever thought about management?"

"No, I really haven't."

"I think you should. I think you'd be good at it. I've been talking to the owner and the other managers, and they agree with me. You're at a great place here. This is a high-profile restaurant. We do thirteen million dollars a year. You could do worse."

"Thank you so much, Ernie, but I'm just not ready to give up on my dream."

He smiled and shook his head, like he was thinking, *Oh my God, this poor deluded kid.* But he said, "Just think about it."

CHAPTER EIGHT

SERVICE

Let each of you look out not only for his own interests, but also for the interests of others. – Philippians 2:4

My talent for defiant independence was only matched by my respect for capable authority, so when Ernie, the general manager, said, "Think about it," I did. For a long time. Back then, I didn't know why I hesitated. But I know now. I was afraid.

Everything I had tried in my life to that point, I had failed. Everyone I had loved seemed to die or give up, and this had somehow gotten bound up with my picture of myself as a failure. Every time I considered the possibility I might *not* fail, that scared me even more. What if I was good at it? People might expect something of me. Once I let that happen, there was no turning back. If I succeeded, the opportunities to fail would just get bigger, make it possible to fall farther. Those kinds of thoughts kept me circling around that decision for weeks. Maybe if I waited long enough, Ernie would forget he had ever dangled the opportunity in front of me.

On the other hand, once he put the idea in my head, it would not let go. Every time I tried to think about the dream I claimed I had—to be an actor—I couldn't help thinking about how I enjoyed spending my actual time: supporting and hanging out with my co-workers, going above and beyond to impress my managers, keeping my customers laughing.

I had stumbled into my first dishwashing job for lack of a better idea or a better education. I barely graduated high school. I didn't go to college. I was a flunky who had learned the restaurant business by flunking out of restaurant jobs over and over and over again, and by being given a second chance, a third, a fourth. I never forgot that I'd started as a dishwasher, and never failed to say hello and shoot the breeze with the dishwashers and bussers every day when I clocked in.

I thought I wanted to be an actor because of my natural talent for entertaining people, but the service industry gave me a chance to entertain people without the distance of a stage or screen, to serve a great night directly to our clientele. I was a natural at creating relationships, with customers, fellow employees, vendors, managers, whoever entered the bar. That was my theater.

This whole time, while I'd been biding my time in restaurants waiting to figure out what I wanted to do, I had grown to love what I was already doing. It felt like my future had surrounded me, and I was just now seeing it.

I knocked on Ernie's door. "Hey Ernie. I've thought about it. I want to do it."

"Do what?"

"Management."

"Of course you do."

What did he see in me despite all my efforts to be a clown? I was only 23 and still living with my dad, so I could hardly have put my finger on it then. But I know now what I see in others who remind me of the guy I was back then: an outgoing personality, a competitive streak, a willingness to do whatever it took to solve a problem, and pride in my work ethic. It was like once I removed drugs from the equation, a fog lifted and I saw myself not only as I was but as I could be.

Once I latched onto the idea of management, shooting for that goal became my passion. What happened next? Almost nothing. This was not a restaurant chain with a management training program. This was an independent restaurant with a single owner. "Management training" meant "learn as you go."

The first thing the GM did was give me a new title, assistant bar manager, which meant I pretty much did the same thing I was already doing, for longer hours and less pay. Instead of serving drinks until we closed, I was the first bartender cut from behind the bar every night. So, at 10:00 or so, I would stop getting tips, but I still had to stay until closing. I'd change into a manager's uniform, count inventory, and help close up. I was "in charge" of the bar. Mostly I was the monkey with the keys. Once in a while, I made decisions to comp a drink, cut off a customer, or tell a bartender to clock out early because it was slow. I never received a formal evaluation. Instead, now and then one of the managers would say, "You're doing a great job." That was my training program.

***

Where I had once become an expert at using alcohol and drugs to escape, managing at a place that *served* alcohol taught me one of my greatest lessons in personal responsibility. A couple of nights before Christmas, I was working behind the bar, when a bar-back who was off work brought his girlfriend in for a drink. A bar-back

is a guy who runs support for the main bartenders: washing glasses, restocking booze, loading kegs, cleaning the bar. He wasn't a
bartender, but he knew the rules. He knew bartenders can be held
liable for over-serving, even if the people they serve have already
had a head start before they come in. Thing is, it's not always easy
to tell at a glance if people are on their way to drunk.

This bar-back and his girlfriend had already been drinking
when they came in and ordered two beers. I served them. Shortly
after that, the other bartender and I saw signs they were drunk:
bodies swaying, words slurring, eyes not tracking. I walked over
and said, "Hey, no more for you," took their beers away, and cut
them off. But none of us on shift went the extra step to call them a
cab. They left the bar, got in his car, and hit the road.

The bar-back came to an intersection where a young father was
sitting at a stoplight, and when the bar-back's light turned red he
didn't notice. The young father's light turned green, and he pulled
out. The bar-back T-boned the other guy's car, crushing his body
in a tangle of metal. He survived for about ten days before he died.

The bar-back was charged with reckless homicide and aggra-
vated driving under the influence. In turn, the victim's family and
the bar-back sued us, for over-serving him. It didn't matter that I
only served him a single beer and took it away before he finished.
We were legally responsible.

The lawsuit got settled out of court, but I never forgot that co-
worker, or the man he killed. I still picture it often: two young guys
who never met, one enjoying a night out with his girl, the other
heading home to his kid, all of us looking forward to Christmas,
and then in an instant all our fates colliding in that intersection.
Was it the half a beer I served him that put him over the top?
Would it have happened anyway? What if we had called him a cab?

There's no way to know. I only know I felt responsible, and I never wanted it to happen again.

I still tell that story to people all the time, whether they're in the restaurant business or not: "All you've got to do is serve somebody one drink, even if you don't know where they've been or what they've been doing, even if you cut them off. If they get in a car and kill somebody, it's on you. Maybe you think I'm telling you this because of the lawsuit and all the money it cost the restaurant. But that wasn't the worst of it. The truth is: a man lost his life, and his family will never be whole again. I have to live with that for the rest of my life. And I don't want that to happen to you."

The GM understood this was one of the costs of running a business that involves daily judgment calls that can impact people's lives. Despite my mistake, avoidable or not, he never lost faith in my ability to juggle our promise to give customers a special experience with our responsibility to protect the health and safety of everyone we served. It wouldn't be the last judgment call I made that reminded me that the word "service," in or out of the service industry, means so much more than just handing someone what they ask for.

***

One day the dining room manager moved on, so the GM said, "You've been doing such a great job in the bar, how would you like to manage the dining room?" I was still a monkey with keys, but with one less manager to report to.

I'd only been managing the dining room for a couple of weeks, when I faced my next unexpected crisis, this time during a lunch rush. I was walking through the dining room to see how everything was going when a woman customer bolted up from her table, alternately flailing her arms and clutching her throat, but saying nothing. It so happened I had finished a first aid training session less than a week before, and it was clear from her silence and the emerging blue shade to her face that she was choking.

The restaurant was a renovated barn, so the dining room had a wide-open floor plan, and the place was packed with some 300 customers watching in horror. Maybe a dozen rose from nearby tables as if ready to leap into action, but I was already spinning the woman around to face away from me. I wrapped my arms around her torso, clasped my hands together, and punched upward against her solar plexus, creating the maximum amount of air pressure I could to pop out whatever was in her throat. And...

Nothing.

I knew the first push was most important, that if the object didn't come out the first time it might lodge deeper. But I did it again, determined to make the second time count, and this time an olive catapulted across the room. She sputtered as the whole room broke into applause. Then she gave me a big hug. I thought, *Cool, two weeks on the job and I already saved somebody's life. This is all right.*

The image of the intersection where the bar-back and the father collided faded a little bit.

A week later, this time during a dinner rush, I walked through the dining room when a lady fell out of her chair onto the floor. She was not clutching her throat, but her chest. She was having a heart attack. A man ran up from another table and announced he was a doctor. He checked her pulse. There was none. Together we did CPR: him blowing air into her lungs, and me doing chest compressions.

Fewer than twenty percent of people who suffer cardiac arrest outside a hospital survive, even with CPR. That number drops to five percent if you check back on those patients a month later. But we got lucky. The woman survived. The City of South Barrington, Illinois honored me with an award for saving not one, but two lives in their community.

I didn't have any illusions that these chances to come to the rescue made me some sort of angel. Still, I felt pretty satisfied with myself, thinking I must be good at this hero business. Working in management was giving me a bigger chance to be a superstar than acting.

***

I never saved a customer's life again. As time went on, my real talent became clear, the one that had prompted my mother to call me her little preacher: I could talk my way into or out of anything.

The management never talked about my special skill. Nobody had to. Once they put me in the dining room, I could resolve any employee problem or any customer complaint. My mom had always had a gift for making people happy to be wherever she was, and I felt like she walked that floor with me. The right words or actions always just came to me, not only to get things moving forward again but to make people happy with the results. I never had to lie or fake anything to achieve that. I honestly cared about serving.

In customer service, I learned quickly that most people simply want to have a voice and be heard, to be shown compassion and care, and to have their problems resolved quickly with as little fuss as possible. The key was finding out what people really wanted and doing my best to give it to them, or at least meet them halfway. I never found any of that hard to do.

One day, a food server walked up to me and said, "Hey, Keith, will you go talk to Table Eighteen?" I neglected to ask the waiter the backstory, just walked up to the table, standing tall, full of my authority as dining room manager. It was a table full of guys, so I was on alert for the smells and signs of alcohol.

But all I said was, "Hey, how we doing? Is there something I can help you with?"

One guy said, "I don't know, are you a dentist?"

My stomach sank as I thought, oh man, this guy's going to give me a hard time. "What happened?"

He continued to be sarcastic. "You tell me. I'm having a Caesar salad, which is normally a pretty safe activity as far as my teeth are concerned. So, you tell me, what can possibly be in a Caesar salad that can chip a tooth?"

"I don't know, sir. There shouldn't be anything in there that can do that. I'd like to help make it right though."

But he was on a roll, and now his friends joined in, "So you're going to fix his tooth for him?"

I knew they were trying to make me feel foolish. I'd been in plenty of fights in Conroe, and they had taught me one thing: when guys are raring for a fight, the best thing to do is to let them get whatever's bugging them off their chest, listen thoroughly, and acknowledge their right to be angry. I also knew I had to take responsibility for solving his problem without automatically accepting guilt, fault, or blame in any legal issue that might lead to a lawsuit.

I let them tease me for a while before I said, "Look, I'm sorry, I really am trying to be nice, guys. And I really am willing to solve this." I said something to indicate I realized he had come in to enjoy a meal with friends, not to end up in pain in a dentist's chair. Then I offered to comp their meal and had them fill out an accident report. Mostly though, I listened and let him talk until he was all talked out, commiserated with him, and even told a story of my own. By the time we wrapped up, we were all laughing.

We never did figure out what he bit into, though there weren't too many possibilities: an eggshell, crouton, or maybe a tiny rock from a piece of lettuce that had not been thoroughly cleaned. There was a remote possibility it was something else floating around the kitchen. The important thing was, I let the customer be right without making the restaurant wrong.

That guy sent a nice letter to my general manager complimenting me for the professional way I handled the situation. Here's what he liked: I was calm, I listened, I did everything possible to resolve the situation, and I followed up by passing the issue up the chain to make sure the general manager followed up.

Although it worked out, I realized afterward that if I had it to do again I would do it differently. The first thing I had learned about conflict, back in Conroe when I hung out with guys carrying guns, was this: you can avoid a lot of fights if you ask for the backstory before you ever show up to confront someone. This eliminates some of the surprise that can throw you off guard and make it hard to control the urge to grow defensive. It also gives you more time to anticipate solutions. I needed to remember to apply this in the restaurant.

The next time a server asked me to talk to a customer, I asked them to first give me the full story as they understood it. After that, I still asked the customer to explain the problem, but I was a lot more prepared to offer solutions.

Regardless of how things turned out with each obstacle I encountered, one constant remained: I stayed calm and good-humored under pressure. I came to see that this was a skill important to any leader, in or out of the service industry. After all, leading is always about serving. My mother had taught us kids that when she taught us about Jesus. And just because I stopped believing in God, didn't mean I stopped believing in the importance of serving others.

As I grew in my new vocation, my fear of failure didn't go away, I just stopped letting it be a factor in my decisions. By taking on the challenge of management, I learned a powerful truth: that acting above our fears is the only path to discovering our true destiny in life.

***

Being a good manager was not enough to take me to the top at that restaurant. I reached a point where it was going to be tough to climb farther. There were about eight assistant managers under the general manager, and I was maybe sixth in the succession.

Ernie inspired loyalty, and most of the managers who worked under him had been there for years. That meant it could take me years to move up. As for Ernie, he wasn't going anywhere. If I wanted to become a general manager, I'd have to wait for him to retire. He was only in his forties. His retirement was decades away.

Soon two young hotshots became regulars, and one day these guys told me they had landed a loan to start a new restaurant and brewery, from the ground up. They offered me a job as assistant GM, on the spot, no interview required.

I did not try to fake confidence I didn't have. "That's a pretty big jump. Not sure I have the experience you're looking for."

"Not true. We've seen you in action and we like how you operate. We want you. We're willing to pay you big. You're going to be our guy."

Despite my warnings that I was nowhere near ready, they offered me twice what I was making. They wanted me to help them have a new place up and running in five months, less than half the time a project that big normally requires, but I didn't know that back then. I didn't know anything about starting a restaurant from scratch.

"Okay, I'm in."

CHAPTER NINE

THE GRAND OPENING

Then the Lord God said, "It is not good that the man should be alone; I will make him a helper fit for him." – Genesis 2:18

Although I had no experience opening a new restaurant, that wasn't the painful part of my new job. What made it painful was that the new owners of the Prairie Rock Brewing Company had no restaurant experience at all but still insisted on being hands-on. They wanted in on every phase of the operation.

The concept was cool. They built a restaurant and microbrewery in an old silent movie theatre. The inside had been gutted, leaving behind a vast space they turned into a dining room that would seat 450. That should have been a winning plan. Plenty of seating is one of the top signs of a restaurant with staying power. Then I saw the kitchen they were building, and I had a sinking realization these guys had no idea what they were doing. Their contractors were constructing a kitchen that felt tight as a shoebox, too small to create meals for a small bistro, much less a 450-seat dining room. It was the smallest commercial kitchen I've ever seen.

The owners were everywhere, excited about their plans. But the moment I saw my chance for a moment alone with the general manager, I pulled her aside and said, "No way is that kitchen going to work. You know it, I know it, the chef knows it. Can't you make them see that?"

She told me she had tried, but the owners insisted it was just part of working with a historical building and we had to make it work. I was young enough and new enough at this that I hoped maybe they knew something I didn't. After all, the owners convinced someone to give them a loan for this place. I did as I was told and kept my nose in my own department: developing the menu, meeting with the brewmaster to build a beer list, creating a wine list, ordering smallwares, ordering product.

I was also in charge of interviewing, hiring, and training staff. I enjoyed identifying in others those people skills that were my specialty. A lot of people claim to like working with people, but top-notch service requires reading and responding to customers at an intuitive level. It's kind of like a dance, where the customer takes the lead, but really the servers are anticipating things to the point that there's almost a telepathic conversation going on.

One prospective hire was so good at this, I didn't notice until after our interview that she seemed to be interviewing me almost as much as I was interviewing her. Not an interrogation, just a show of genuine interest in learning what qualities and values were important to me as a manager. I usually did my best to make job applicants feel at ease, but it seemed like she was the one making me feel at ease, so I knew she would be great at making customers feel that way too.

I also knew I would have to be careful around her, because she was drop-dead gorgeous.

Dating between management and employees is generally frowned on in the restaurant business because it opens up the risk of lawsuits, not to mention awkward situations: power struggles,

ANCHORED *by* GRACE

favoritism, or people just quitting when relationships don't work out. There's often a lot of drinking and partying among restaurant employees, and the potential for trouble can be high. But I figured Chicago was a big city with plenty of pretty girls, and I had no problem landing dates. I decided I simply wouldn't ask out the pretty new waitress. No problem.

One night shortly before we opened for business, a couple of friends and I went to a country-music bar in the city, and there she was: Annette, and a couple of her friends. She smiled and waved. I waved back, but didn't walk over to say hello. I stuck with my friends at the bar, keeping my distance. Every time I glanced in her direction I got the feeling she had just turned away so I wouldn't catch her looking at me. Then the band went on break, and the DJ played a slow one by Rick Trevino, "I Only Get This Way With You." Did she know he was from Texas and remember I was too? It seemed rude to say no after she walked all the way across the bar to ask me to dance. In any case, I could not resist an open invitation to put my arms around this beautiful woman with the warmest smile I'd ever seen.

The minute we stepped onto the dance floor together, it was like we had been born to move in sync, and we didn't need any music to know it. I felt the little bit of air between us turn warm with certainty: she was already my girl, whether either of us thought it was a good idea or not. Every point of contact was driving me nuts: her right hand in my left, my right hand on the small of her back, her hair under my cheek.

I escorted her back to her friends and said, "You know, I'd love to ask you out."

She grinned. "Then, why don't you?"

"Because I'm a manager and you're an employee. We're not supposed to date."

But next time I saw her, I asked myself, *Why not, Keith? This restaurant is a losing proposition anyway. It's never getting off the ground, and you know it.* So, one evening during a break in a staff training session, I pulled her aside and asked her to meet me after work, at a late-night bar that served until 4:00 a.m.

"I thought you said we're not supposed to date," she said.

"We're not."

Her grin was irresistible. Oh man, was I in trouble.

We met at the after-hours bar, sat at a table, and just talked. I felt awkward at first. What was I thinking? But she dove right into asking me all about myself like it was the most natural thing in the world, until I felt like we were just picking up where we left off in a conversation we had already been having all our lives. That night, I told her all about my mom, which was kind of weird because I wasn't the type to open up about anything, much less that agonizing subject.

She learned a lot more about me than I did about her that night, but I didn't need to know much to know it was right. I did find out she was a schoolteacher by day, and took the waitressing job to supplement a tight income. It didn't take long to get that she was that sort of patient teacher who made every kid feel like he was her favorite. But something told me that with me, that feeling wasn't just a fantasy. It was real.

In the two weeks leading up to opening night, we went out several times. We crossed the line, but that line was not made for us. She was a year older than me, and I joked with her that she was "contributing to the delinquency of a minor." We agreed not to tell anyone.

***

Opening night at Prairie Rock, just as I predicted, our tiny kitchen could not turn orders around in anything resembling a timely fashion. It was nowhere near equipped to deal with the creative menu the owners demanded. The executive chef and his staff fell further and further behind.

I overheard the chef tell the GM, "I warned you this kitchen did not have enough room to handle this menu."

When the GM left, the chef turned to me and said, "I'm so out of here." He didn't leave right then, but the threat hung there all night long.

Customers were waiting two hours for food. We were only halfway through our first night and I already knew: I was done. I might not have known what I was doing when they hired me, but I knew I was way better at this than they were. I walked through the dining room, and a customer who looked ticked off kept trying to catch my eye as I moved toward his section, while I desperately tried to avoid eye contact. The whole room was growling and surly, and I knew if I stopped I would become a target for everyone within hearing distance.

Finally, the customer called out, "Hey, man, are you one of the managers?"

I turned to him like I wasn't sure he meant me and said, "No. I'm just on my way to the bathroom," and kept going, pretending I was another customer like him.

The next day I told one of the partners, "I don't think this is going to work for me."

"Oh, Keith, I know we had some opening-night snags, but that's not unusual."

"You sure about that? I mean, opening night is when you're supposed to put your best foot forward."

"Give it time. We'll get better at this."

"I don't see how it's going to change unless you guys get out of the way and let me and the other managers run things. You guys know about landscaping and development. But we know about restaurants. You've got to let the experts run this."

"You see! We're already growing. A few months ago, you told me you were no expert."

He wasn't listening.

That night the waiting list grew to three hours long, but it didn't faze me anymore because in my mind I was already applying at another restaurant, taking a job as a bartender again if I had to. Then, as I walked through the impatient crowd waiting in the bar, I saw a familiar face, one of the former partners from my previous restaurant.

He smiled, waved, and gave his chin a little jerk. "Keith, come over here!"

I pushed through several people to reach him and shook his hand. "Hey, Scott, good to see you!"

"I heard you left the old place. So, this is what you're doing?" Scott grinned like he was biting his tongue.

"Yeah, I'll admit it's kinda rough. But we're working out our stuff." I knew he knew this was the understatement of the year, but I also knew it was poor form to bad-mouth an employer.

He gave a philosophical nod that suggested he knew it wasn't my fault. "Yeah, seems like it. Listen, my partners and I are doing a deal with Walter Payton, and we'd love for you to come over."

"Walter Payton? The Hall of Fame running back for the Chicago Bears?"

"Yeah, we think his name will be a big boost. But the location's great too. We bought this eighty-thousand-square-foot roundhouse in Aurora, and I'd like to show you around and see if you'd be interested." He leaned in. "It's got a great kitchen. Would you come by and talk to us?"

I saw no point in playing coy. We both knew which way this place was headed. So, I said, "Sure."

I went to the roundhouse the next day. The moment I walked in, before Scott could give me a tour, before I had time to take in my surroundings, up walked a handsome young black man with a mustache, a couple of inches shorter than me but with broad shoulders. He was a big deal in Chicago, so I would have known his face anywhere. I concentrated on acting casual, or at least as casual as I would with any other potential employer.

He shook my hand. "I understand you're Keith Isbell."

"Yeah, I am." I was so star-struck, I had no idea what else to say.

"Well, I'm Walter Payton."

I chuckled. "Yeah, I know who you are. You're the NFL's all-time rushing leader."

"I'm supposed to recruit you." He grinned at Scott, who had obviously said those words to him, but who surely had not told him to use those words on me. "So, what do you say, will you come work here?"

"Okay," I said. Then, "Now that that's settled, mind if I have a look around?"

The roundhouse was ripped down to the bones, but already it was a big beautiful building, with a huge kitchen as promised. These guys were taking their time to get everything right.

I gave two weeks' notice at Prairie Rock.

Right after my final two weeks was up, one of Prairie Rock's managers asked Annette into his office. He got straight to the point. "We understand you dated Keith."

"Yeah, I did."

"Sorry, but we don't allow fraternizing here. You're fired."

"But he doesn't even work here anymore."

"No, but he did when you went out."

He gave her a speech about trust and boundaries, but afterward we both agreed it was obvious they were just ticked because I left two weeks after they opened, and they were so vindictive they took it out on her to get to me. I was doubly ticked off because I knew for a fact one of the partners was having an affair with the other partner's wife.

I told Annette, "I have half a mind to tell his buddy."

"It's sweet you want to defend me," Annette said, "but why make more bad blood? I hated that job anyway, and they'll pay the price soon enough. That place is going under."

She said it was for the best, because she realized she couldn't wait tables and give the focus she wanted to give to her teaching. Doing both was exhausting.

We were right about Prairie Rock. It didn't last a year. Those guys took it right over a cliff.

***

I never regretted working at Prairie Rock, because if it hadn't been for that terrible place I wouldn't have met Annette, the greatest woman I'd ever known since my mother. She was not merely beautiful, funny, and smart. All those things would have caught my attention, but those things alone would not have held it.

Annette was thoughtful in a way I had not experienced with any other woman I'd dated. She not only asked a lot of questions and listened to the answers, she also listened for the meaning.

She could tell by the way I talked about Texas that I was always a little homesick. She could tell by the way I talked about my friends in Chicago that I liked them, but that there was a part of me that always felt a little lonely. She did not ask me vague questions about family, friends, and home, but wanted to know every story inside and out: the kind of love I once had in my life that made me believe in family and how it felt to lose that, the kind of friends who went beyond hanging out drinking beer and laughing to show the kind of loyalty that made them my second family, the sense of belonging to a place almost as if it were a living breathing person.

This special kinship with Annette worked both ways. She brought out the more selfless side of me, the me that wanted to be a better man, the man my mother had believed I could be. I had always taken an interest in people, but I wanted to know Annette in a way I had never known anyone else. Her answers went as deep as her questions. She didn't merely tell me funny and sad stories about her life, but also revealed how the dynamics of her family worked: why she was not close to her sister even though she loved her, what about her parents she wanted to emulate and which of their mistakes she wanted to avoid, which friendships stood the test of time and why.

I had never before experienced such a complete exchange with another human being. Talking with Annette, feeling so completely heard, helped heal every wound I'd picked up along the way: the death of my mother, the shattering of my family, almost losing myself in drugs and booze. I never was a touchy-feely guy, but with her it was okay. It was safe. I had never had that before. The total acceptance she gave me was powerful. In return, I loved her on every level. I could already see her as an understanding wife and supportive partner. I could already see her as an adoring mother who would raise happy, self-confident children.

I knew she was the woman for me. Within six months, I asked her to move in.

I wanted to give her the best, even then, and that meant my utilitarian bachelor apartment would not cut it. We looked for a rental house in Aurora, Illinois, so we could be close to my work at Walter Peyton's Roundhouse. I worked longer hours than Annette, and the shorter my drive to and from work the more time we could spend together.

Rents were high in Aurora, so when we found a great place at a low price we didn't question why. Annette and I were just excited to start our new life together.

CHAPTER TEN

PRANKSTERS

Iron sharpens iron, So one man sharpens another. - Proverbs 27:17

I prided myself on being a sensible guy, who had not only rejected God as a fantasy, but also refused to believe anything that could not be explained by logic, reason, or observation. For me, there was no such thing as an afterlife, spirits, ghosts, poltergeists, or paranormal phenomena. I was certain those ideas were ridiculous. In spite of that, I had no doubt our rental house was haunted. Maybe not by ghosts, maybe by some phenomenon science will one day explain—though I doubt it—but definitely invaded by something beyond the world I knew.

Our house was not merely an old and creaky place with character. The events we experienced inside that dwelling were impossible to explain away as wind or magnetics or settling earth. Whatever the house was, or whatever lived in it with us, it did not just visit at night or when one of us was alone, so it was hard to chalk up to paranoia or phobia. If a house could ever be declared crazy, then this was the place.

My first full day in the house, it let me know it wanted me out of there. I turned a corner into our bedroom, where across from our queen-size bed sat a dresser with a CD player on top. Just as I walked in, the player ejected the CD and shot it halfway across the room at such high velocity it landed in the middle of the bed. I didn't dare stop or turn to look at any of it. It seemed important to keep walking and pretend I didn't see anything. No way that was real, I told myself. I had a weird feeling someone was there with me. No way I was acknowledging that either. That would be like admitting I was losing my mind, or worse, admitting there were things in this world even further beyond my control than I thought.

Not long after that I was in the bathroom, sitting on the throne minding my own business, when something caught my eye. *Oh my God, what is that?* I thought. There on the shelf directly across from me, Annette's hairbrush lifted itself from horizontal to vertical, dragged across the shelf, and fell to the floor.

That was only the beginning.

In the coming months, that house came alive; we saw objects dragged or thrown or knocked over, we heard footsteps when we were both sitting and nobody else was in the house, we passed through pockets of cold air or they passed through us, we felt creepy sensations of being watched, even stalked. Bear, our German Shepherd-Husky mix, acted terrorized half the time. Sometimes I'd find him backed into a corner, hair on his neck standing up, barking as if at an invisible intruder.

I went to the library to look up information on our address, to find out if strange events had ever been reported there—involving humans, ghosts, or otherwise. Nothing came up.

Annette dealt with more spooky encounters than I did because I worked long hours and was rarely home. I would call her on my break and ask, "So, what did our ghost do today?"

"I was sitting at the kitchen table and Bear's bone got dragged off the floor about four feet," she said.

"Are you all right?"

"Oh yeah, I'm fine. It was just weird."

I knew this levelheaded woman was the one for me, because she was already aces in the for-better-or-worse department. I just felt guilty that, despite being a manager who worked some eighty hours a week, I didn't make enough money to buy us a new house without devious spirits.

A couple of nights she called me to say something like, "Somebody's walking up and down the stairs. I can hear their footsteps, loud and clear. I'm scared this time someone's actually in the house." Our place was five minutes away, and she sounded so freaked out I rushed home, only to arrive and find nobody else there besides Annette.

We laughed about it, how we were the proud owners of a dog and a poltergeist, how if we had kids we wouldn't have to hire a babysitter because the ghost could watch them, how it wouldn't be so bad if we could charge this roommate rent. But underneath the jokes, we hated that house.

In spite of the anxiety of living with an unwelcome guest, he never got between us. We faced these and other problems with the determination that everything would work out if we kept our sense of humor and got through it together. I asked Annette to marry me, and she swore to never take off her ring lest our invisible roomie swipe it. Our first decision as an engaged couple was, "Baby, let's get the hell out of here and let the ghost have the house to himself."

I called the landlord. "Look, we're outta this place. I don't think this ghost, or whatever it is, is evil like it's trying to scare us. But it's way too playful and I'm tired of my door being knocked on at 3:00 a.m. every night. I can't sleep." That's right, this thing, whatever it was, had taken to rapping on the door, *bup-bup-bup*, every night at the same time. Annette heard it too. I would go to answer the door, and nobody would be there. If it was kids playing ding-dong-ditch, then they were stealthier and more persistent than any delinquents in history. I never heard anyone running from the house, just that rap on the door night after night until whatever it was drove us out.

Six months later, Annette and I moved to an apartment. Recently, I looked up our old address on Google Earth just out of curiosity. The property owner had leveled the house. All that was left was an empty lot. My guess is nobody else was willing to stay in that old place either.

***

Even though my new job came with more responsibilities, it paid less than my previous one, but I didn't mind. I saw managing this massive facility as a proving ground where I would get the kind of on-the-job training to launch a successful career. What's more, I was working for football hero Walter freaking Payton.

The Roundhouse was on the National Register of Historic Places. The complex included a rotating structure where the trains that once ran on the old Chicago and Aurora Railroad used to get hooked up, rotated off the tracks, and sidelined so mechanics could work on them. The place was falling apart before Scott and his wife partnered up with investors, brought in Walter Payton, and con-vinced the City of Aurora it would be to the town's benefit to sell them the property to rehabilitate and turn into a local attraction.

The place was already a marvel, a big donut-shaped structure with a 20,000-square-foot open-air gazebo in the middle. We opted to offer outdoor dining, drinking, and entertainment in the gazebo. The indoor dining room was multilevel, and included a banquet facility. The kitchen was big enough to service it all.

Scott made it clear he wanted me on board because he saw me as a decision maker, a "wild brain" as I call it, someone who knows how to create ideas from thin air and turn them into reality. He trusted me to set this place apart from other restaurants. Succeeding at that would set *me* apart from other managers.

With that in mind, I was fearless about laying my dream scenarios out for Scott even before we opened. "You know, Scott, I love to golf, and I'm here almost every waking hour, and this place is so big. Boy, it would be nice while we're doing training and construction, if we could put in a putting green to blow off a little steam. I think it'll also make a great attraction when we open."

He grinned like he was not sure if I was kidding, but also like it didn't matter if I was or not because anything that made both of us smile that big would likely have the same effect on customers. It ended up being one of the most fun parts of the complex after we opened, a hot-spot for entertainment. They kept the putting green long after I left.

Once Scott okayed my first idea, it grew easier to spring more on him: "I think we have an opportunity to cut the cost on our linens by doing our laundry in-house."

"Whatever that means, all right," he said. "If it'll save us money, go for it."

So, I cancelled our laundry service, bought a washer and dryer plus two tables for folding, hired two workers to do laundry full time, and set them all up in a back room. That move cut our laundry costs substantially. More important, it taught me that good ideas only come to life if we put action behind them.

My best moneymaker was my unique approach to Super Bowl Sunday. That's usually a busy day for bars but a down day for restaurants.

I said, "Let's turn the whole Roundhouse into one big bar."

Steve said, "And how do you propose we do that?"

I could see it all in my head: we would order extra everything for the three bars we already had, set up a few separate temporary stations for beer (the most popular drink at any Super Bowl party), hire a DJ for the second level, rig a balloon drop, ask several staff members to loan us TVs to hook up all over the restaurant, and, the crowning glory, rent a jumbo screen for the main bar. This was back in the early nineties, before flat screens were common. We hired a local movie company to hook everything up. We charged twenty bucks a person to get in the door, and we packed the place. Those Super Bowl parties continued for almost two decades, until another company bought The Roundhouse in 2011.

Year-round, The Roundhouse offered multiple options to turn an evening out into an event: a microbrewery, a cognac cigar bar, an oyster champagne bar, a Walter Payton museum featuring all his NFL memorabilia, and, of course, the chance to spot Walter himself on the premises.

***

I loved it when Walter came in because he lent the place his down-to-earth, fun-loving attitude. Meanwhile, I suspect he liked that I didn't fall on my knees to kiss his leather shoes but instead treated him like any of my other bosses, with friendly respect.

Before we first opened, he asked me to help him put his museum together. I couldn't help feeling he was having a little fun at my expense, running me up and down a ladder moving his trophies around and around.

At one point he said, "Nah, I don't like that trophy there. Drop it down over here."

I didn't realize that trophy had two parts—the base and the statue—so I grabbed it by the base, and the glass football on top fell off, hit the ground, and chipped. I looked down from the ladder in horror.

But he said, super casual, "Hey, man, pick that up."

I climbed down the ladder, picked it up, and read the inscription. "Dude, this is your all-time NFL rushing trophy!"

"Yeah, don't worry about it. It was propping a door open at home. Just put it over there."

That attitude was the main reason I respected Walter as an example of the kind of leadership I wanted to emulate. Not because he was an NFL star, but because he was authentic with people.

One weekend night at the Roundhouse, we got a call from a guy who said, "I'm with Kenny Rogers and I'd like to place an order." He ordered five grilled-cheese sandwiches and three Diet Cokes. The hostess who took the call came to me to make sure she responded correctly. She didn't want to fall for a prank, but also didn't want to fall down on service by telling a legit customer we couldn't fill that order because those items weren't on our menu. Which they weren't. I thought the order sounded odd, but I figured Kenny Rogers had as much of a right to enjoy comfort food as anybody. "No big deal," I said. "We can do it." I told her to put the order in. I also told her I'd personally deliver it.

I'll admit, I didn't have to do that, but: 1) I thought sending a manager over with the delivery was the right touch for a high-profile customer, and 2) I was excited to meet one of the most famous stars to ever top the charts in both country and pop music.

Walter was in the house, so I found him and said, kind of breathless, "Kenny Rogers just placed an order and I'm gonna run it over to him. Wanna come with me?"

I couldn't believe his response. "Kenny who?"

I spoke slower, "Kenny Rogers, man! *The Gambler*? The country singer?"

He shrugged, indicating he had no idea what I was talking about, but he said, "All right, I'll go with you."

The moment the grilled cheeses came off the grill, I packed up the food, Walter and I jumped in my car, and I drove us to Rogers' hotel down the street. Inside the hotel, we hopped in the elevator, and the moment the doors closed, while I was still trying to explain who Kenny Rogers was, Walter cut loose a loud fart. I saw him stifling laughter and knew he did it to prank me, passing gas in an enclosed space. Then his face changed, and it was clear the stench took him by surprise too. It was one of the most horrible sensory experiences of my life.

I said, "Oh my God, dude, what is wrong with you?"

He laughed harder. My eyes were watering, but I laughed too, at the hilarious horror of being stuck with him until the tenth floor. Worse, the elevator stopped at eight. I thought, *oh no, please don't let anyone get on.* The doors opened to reveal an old woman who had to be at least in her eighties.

Her eyes widened when she saw Walter. "Oh my gosh, Walter Payton!"

"Hi!" he said. "Going up?"

"Down," she said, and I exhaled in relief. Then she said, "But that's okay, I don't mind waiting," and got in with us.

The doors closed. *Oh no, this poor old woman*, I thought, *and she's going to think it's me!* Because this was the kind of smell that attaches to your clothes. But she cut up with Walter, both of them chuckling, all the while his eyes boring into mine as if to chant, "We-have-a-secret!" Either she couldn't smell anything, or she was so excited to meet Walter she didn't care.

On the tenth floor we got out, but my embarrassment kept going up because even though I had thought it would be cool to present Walter Payton to Kenny Rogers, now it seemed cruel. But as we walked down the corridor, the smell seemed to retreat, and I relaxed.

Rogers did not answer his own door, but I told the guy who did, "I'm Keith Isbell with Walter Payton's Roundhouse, and I've got Walter Payton with me."

"Come on in," he said.

We walked in to see Rogers lying on the couch.

I stepped forward and started introductions. "Hello, Mr. Rogers, I'm..."

Before I could finish, Rogers saw Walter and jumped to his feet. "Oh, my God!"

Walter pumped his hand. "I can't believe I'm standing in the same room as Kenny Rogers."

And Rogers said, "I can't believe I'm standing in the same room as Walter Peyton."

And I said, "I can't believe I'm standing in the same room as both of you guys."

We all had a good chuckle, I got an autograph, and moments later Walter and I left.

On our way back to the restaurant, Walter sang the Kenny Rogers song "Lady." I smirked, not because he was a great singer but because I realized he had known all along who Kenny Rogers was. After he sang a few bars, he asked, "What do you think?"

I said, "Don't quit your day job."

The next day, a reporter called from the local paper. "I hear you were with Kenny Rogers and Walter Payton last night."

"Oh, yeah."

"You mind telling me a little bit about it?"

What did I know? I started right in and described the entire scene, minus the bit about the elevator flatulence, shooting my trap off: *blah, blah, blah.* I finished the story with, "I got to listen to Walter Peyton sing 'Lady.'"

The reporter asked, "What was your reaction to that?"

"I told him don't quit his day job."

The reporter thought that was hilarious, and I felt pretty pleased with myself.

The next day, I went in to work and Walter was standing near the entrance waiting for me with a newspaper in his hand. "Let's go talk," he said.

"Okay, sure." I followed him to the banquet room, not thinking anything of it.

The huge room was empty, most of the tables and chairs stashed away. He unfolded the newspaper and pointed at the headline of a celebrity gossip column featuring the story I'd told the reporter about Walter Payton meeting Kenny Rogers, which I'd already seen that morning.

"Did you do that article?" His tone was stern, which was unusual for Walter. For the first time, I worried maybe I had overestimated our relationship.

"Yeah, I did." He knew it was me. I was the only person who'd been with him.

"You can't do that sort of thing without talking to me."

"Okay, sure. I didn't know. Sorry about that." I was thinking, *I'm going to get fired.*

His face got even more serious. "The only part I've got a real issue with is this last part." He pointed at the quote of me saying I had told him not to quit his day job.

"Oh, Walter, that was just a joke."

"No, I know it happened. I remember that. But right here you're saying I can't sing."

"O-kay, yeah…but I was being funny." This was getting weird.

Right then and there he sang "Lady" again, loud, his voice echoing in that giant, empty hall, just the two of us. He finished and asked, "So, what do you think?"

"What do I think?"

"Yeah, how do you think I did?"

I hesitated, confused, wished I could crawl under something. "That sounded very good."

At that moment, a bunch of employees jumped up from the behind the bar where they'd been hiding and burst into laughter and applause.

He had been pulling my leg. Of course.

That article still hangs in my house, a permanent reminder that no matter how successful I become, like Walter I must always keep my sense of humor and never take myself too seriously. To me, those are the marks of humility and humanity, the true ingredients of success.

Walter did more than lead by example. He also gave me good advice. Perhaps the most important was about patience and timing. He saw that I was gung-ho to run off and do my own thing the first chance I got. I'd been at The Roundhouse a few years and, like many ambitious guys in their twenties, I feared falling behind the curve and letting life pass me by. I was thinking, *This is my time.* One day he drew me out, and I admitted I was chomping at the bit to buy my own restaurant.

"You're not ready," he said.

"Okay, but if not now, when?"

"You'll know. When you're ready you won't have to ask. One thing I can tell you: whatever you do, don't do it small, do it big. Until you're ready to do that, be patient."

Although he cautioned me to wait, I saw in the way he treated me that he never doubted I would go big. He only made his appearances at The Roundhouse when I was there, and he always walked the floor with me, happy to share the shine of his stardom, never making me feel like I stood in his shadow.

***

Annette and I decided to have our wedding at The Roundhouse. We agreed it was a smart move for a lot of reasons: it was a fantastic venue, we could use it for free since I worked there, her family and friends lived in Chicago, and my dad and a lot of my friends from the restaurant biz lived there too. The only drawback was that most of my family and friends lived in Conroe and the Houston area, and I was in no position to foot the bill for them. I felt bad about that.

But a bunch of my buddies said, "No problem," rented an RV, and caravanned up.

Seeing them again made me realize how homesick I was for Texas. Time had softened my connection to my old life. One reason I had come north was to get away from influences that had set me on a path of addiction that almost destroyed me. Yet the moment I saw my friends' faces, I could feel that everything had fallen away but the ties of lifelong friendship. A few beers and glasses of champagne revealed there was still a loose cannon or two in the mix, but I was happy to see them too. I knew they had driven so far to throw their arms around me because they wanted me to know they would always have my back.

My wedding day overwhelmed me more than anything had since the day my mother died. That might seem odd to say since I felt as filled with joy on this day as I had felt filled with despair on that one. I guess deep loss had made me wary of life's gifts. It didn't help my anxiety that it poured rain the entire day leading up to our afternoon ceremony. My brother, Kyle, was my best man, and we sat staring from an overhang into the outdoor gazebo, where the ceremony was supposed to take place but which was now effectively the bottom of a waterfall. Staff had moved all the chairs and decorations inside to keep them dry.

"This is terrible," I said.

Kyle didn't try to convince me it wasn't, just tossed an arm across my shoulder. I knew he was thinking about Mom, like I was.

Three minutes before the ceremony was set to begin, the storm broke, the sun came out, and the clouds scattered. My brother walked up to me and said, "Looks like Mom made the wedding."

My friends and family all pitched in to drag chairs and flowers back outside, and the ceremony began. Annette looked so perfect in that golden sunset, I could barely speak. The pastor asked me the usual questions, but it was all I could manage to stutter, "I do."

I think Kyle teased me afterward, something like, "So much for Mom's little preacher." Or maybe he didn't say it out loud, maybe that's just how I read his grin. He didn't talk much that day either, seemed even more nervous than I was.

Kyle was shy as ever, and the idea of the best man's toast had him so terrified he squirmed all day, trying to figure out what to say. At dinner, he was so shaky when he got to his feet I thought, *Oh my gosh, is he going to pass out?* Instead, he gave me a serene smile and said, "The only thing I can think to say, little brother, is this: wasn't it great that Mom made the wedding?" I'm sure he asked everyone to raise a glass to the happy couple, but I heard nothing after the word *Mom*. I didn't need to. In that moment, my brother and I shared an understanding I hadn't felt in years. I knew then that the love we always had for each other had survived.

***

Annette and I only had a few days to go on a honeymoon in Door County, Wisconsin before I was back to walking the floor at The Roundhouse. I had been working at The Roundhouse for several years, but I was still an assistant GM and still working so much I rarely saw my bride. We missed each other the way other people talked about missing lovers in long-distance relationships. I sometimes worked twenty days in a row, double shifts, sixteen hours at a time with no break. That isn't unusual when you're paying your dues. But I was ready to stop paying dues and start reaping rewards. I knew Walter was right; I was not ready to buy a restaurant. But I was ready to take a step in that direction. I needed a shot as a general manager. I also needed to delegate more responsibility so I could work fewer hours. It was time to move on.

I accepted an offer to become the general manager at an Applebee's in Chicago, and gave my notice to The Roundhouse. Walter understood, and I thanked him for all he had taught me.

Not long after that, I was watching the opening pitch of a

Chicago Cubs game when the TV station showed a close-up of Walter in his box seat. He looked sick, downright emaciated, and a local-color commentator made a crack that angered me as much as it saddened me: "Man, he looks like he has AIDS." The word that came to my mind was not AIDS but *cancer*.

Within a day or two, Walter held a press conference to set the record straight. I was right. It was liver cancer.

I called him. "Man, what's going on?"

"It's true," he said. "Just pray for me."

I didn't tell him I was no longer a praying man, just said, "Okay." I did toss up a mental prayer, half of me not believing anyone was listening, the other half hoping that if God was listening, I hadn't burned that bridge.

A couple of weeks later, I was in a friend's wedding at The Roundhouse. Right before the ceremony, one of the restaurant managers walked over and murmured in my ear, "Hey, Keith, come here."

His tone was so heavy I didn't say, but the wedding's about to start. I just followed him to the kitchen. There stood Walter, down eighty pounds, skin hanging off his bones.

He grinned at me. "Hey, what do you think about my diet?"

I smiled back, though I didn't feel it. "Man, it looks like one that works."

"Yeah, I didn't have to do much on this one."

He thrust a small pop-top can in my hand, blue and silver with a picture of a red bull on it. "Hey, can you do me a favor? This company is asking me to advertise their new energy drink, but I really can't drink it. Would you try it and let me know what you think?"

"Sure, anything for you, Walter."

"Oh, and I have something else for you." He gave me a CD with a single song on it. "Why don't you play this for Annette? It's a love song, a good one."

It was. I thanked him and told him I'd get back to him about both. But I never got a chance. He died soon after. That was the last time I saw him.

It was the first time since my mom passed that I knowingly talked to somebody who had cancer, and it hit hard. I knew Walter was a strong man, and to see him dwindled to nothing was a shock. He had helped give me the break I knew would lead to big things and had given me good advice about what to do when I got there. We were not close friends, but he was my mentor. I didn't know that was the word for it back then, but I felt his value.

He was an unforgettable person.

I still remember the day he got me in trouble with Annette. He called and left a voice mail on our answering machine in a high feminine voice: "Keith? I left my panties in your car."

I came home, not knowing about the message, and wondered why she was waiting to pounce on me with the question, "Do you have a girlfriend?"

I listened to the suspect message and laughed. "Oh, that's Walter."

"Sure, it is," she said, like she was only half kidding.

I called him back with Annette standing there. "Hey Walter, did you leave a message on my machine?"

"Yeah..."

"What did you say?"

"That I left my panties in your car."

"You know, Annette heard that, so you need to tell her that was you."

"No, I don't think so."

By the time the call ended, we were all laughing. Walter was a trip.

CHAPTER ELEVEN

CRAZY MANAGERS

Let each of you look out not only for his own interests, but also
for the interests of others. – Philippians 2:4

A buddy who had worked with me at two other restaurants was the guy who convinced me to apply for the general manager's position at Applebee's. "You've got to come here, Keith," Tom said. "We're talking quality of life. They treat their people well, the money's good, and it's a growing company with big upward mobility. They could use someone with your talent."

I had faith in Tom's judgment. I'd known him and his wife since we all started together as bartenders six years earlier. He'd been a groomsman in my wedding. He and his wife hung out with my wife and me. It felt like the perfect way to take the next leap of faith in my career, with a good friend and trusted colleague by my side. I told him, "Sounds good." He recommended me, the bigwigs called me in for an interview, and I aced it. "We'd love to have you on board," the regional manager said, and made me an immediate offer.

Sometime between that offer and my acceptance, I found out Tom was not going to work with me after all. Not ever. He had gotten wind his wife was cheating on him with a close friend. That part didn't surprise me. Tom's wife had cheated before, but he'd given her a second chance. This time, though, he drove to his friend's house, saw his wife's car out front, let himself into the house, and caught them in the act. Here's how a mutual friend told me it went down: "Tom says to her, 'I told you what I'd do if you ever did this to me again.' So, he walks into the guy's kitchen, grabs a knife, and stabs himself in the chest. Then he sits on the floor and dies."

The friend who referred me to Applebee's was dead, and next thing I knew I was at his funeral, one of the most awkward experiences of my life. Everybody there knew the story. I looked into his widow's eyes and could tell she was at a total loss about how to go on from there. I could not imagine how she would ever explain to her boys, who were small at the time, what had happened to their dad. There was nothing right about that day.

A few days later, I started management training at Applebee's, when the group that owned the whole Chicago franchise announced they were selling to another company. Then the new owners assigned me to the store that was the worst performer in the state, possibly the country. So here I was: I had barely walked in the door, the guy who had referred me was dead, the company that had hired me was out, and I was set to manage the biggest loser location in the Chicagoland market.

I spent a couple of sleepless nights, talking to my wife until the wee hours. "I don't know, Annette, I feel like this whole move has been nothing but a series of disasters."

"Or," Annette said, "maybe Tom did you one last favor with that recommendation. Maybe the change in ownership is the first step to a better company. Maybe you'll show them how it's done." Not long after that, Walter Payton died. At that point, it was hard to imagine going back, and Annette convinced me to move forward.

"I bet you'll look back on this new job as one of the smartest moves you ever made."

I told Annette marrying her was the smartest move I ever made. Her faith in me helped me through those early months on the new job.

It wasn't long before my boss sat me down and offered yet another GM position at yet another underperforming, miserable restaurant at the furthest northwest corner of Chicago. I would come to see this was not a punishment but a compliment, a show of faith in my skills: I had a knack for turning around failing restaurants.

***

The moment I arrived at the Northwest Chicago Applebee's, it was clear the three assistant managers considered me the enemy. They had worked there a long time and become tight friends, while I was the outsider who had taken the slot they expected to go to one of them. They all but refused to talk to me.

During our first meeting, they folded their arms at me, smirked, and gave me some version of, "Well, what're we doing?"

I responded by assigning the one with the most experience to run the back of the house, and said I'd run the front of the house until I figured out which departmental responsibilities the other two were best suited for. Then I told one of them, "Guy, first things first: you need to go buy some new shirts." Guy's pit stains were so bad it looked like he'd spilled grease on them! He didn't seem embarrassed by this at all, which concerned me.

That was not my first warning sign Guy was going to be a challenge. My first morning, I noticed that as employees walked through the kitchen to clock in, they all greeted the toaster: "Hi, Guy!... Morning, Guy! How ya doing, Guy?"

"I'm afraid to ask, but why are y'all talking to an appliance?"

"See that spot there on the toaster? That's Guy's burnt skin," one young man explained.

"How'd that get there?"

"Guy head-butted the toaster," he said.

A couple of bystanders laughed.

"It was awesome. He hit it so hard that dark lumpy flesh spot is never coming off. Now every morning we pay our respects."

I was young too, and I knew about blowing off steam. But in the days to come, Guy did nothing to indicate he was willing or able to do anything besides show up. He made a point to do as little as possible for me, the enemy. If I could not convince my managers to manage, I knew this would reflect poorly on me as the new GM, so I had to solve that problem pronto.

I spent my first few days scoping the hourly employees to see who was buying into me and my message: the ones who worked hard, responded well to direction, and acted eager for responsibility. I noticed two young bartenders, Trent and Sean, were organized, respectful to me, and got along great with coworkers and customers alike. I pulled them aside one day after lunch and said, "Hey, what do you guys want to be when you grow up?"

They both said some version of "I want to move into management someday."

"Cool. I think I can help you out with that."

I knew putting bartenders in charge of the bar would help rein in costs. That's because I had learned from experience that bartenders, who make most of their money from tips, tend to overpour and give away free drinks. I figured, make a bartender responsible for all the bar's financial results and that will give the bartender an incentive to protect his department's bottom line. It worked. Trent and Sean quickly turned out to be the best bar managers in the company. I found two other employees to support the kitchen, make truck orders, and maintain smallwares.

Most important, I found the right person to take on my first innovation as a GM.

I had noticed we were losing customers each night because the flow of guests in and out of the dining room was chaos. Every night we had some confused teenager stand up front with a crayon and a blank sheet of paper, guessing wait times. Sometimes the dining room was half empty, yet we still had a twenty-minute wait. These kids had no idea how to manage the restaurant in sections, how to organize the bus staff, or how long it took to turn a table. So, I went to an office supply store, bought a podium, and pulled aside one of our best food servers, Megan.

"Megan, what do you want to do in this business?"

"I want to be a manager."

"Perfect! Come here. I bought this podium at Office Depot. You and I are going to decorate it and outfit it with a seating chart. Then I'm going to teach you how to manage the floor. Then I'm going to put you in a manager's shirt and you're going to run the podium every night." I knew this would cost her tips so I gave her a small raise. That raise could never match her tips, but she saw an opportunity to get a jump-start in management and grabbed it with gratitude.

All the people I handed management responsibilities to were servers, bartenders, and cooks. I bypassed the middlemen, those assistant managers who refused to do anything I said, and instead went directly to the workers, people I could impact the most by giving them opportunities to advance.

In return, I committed to meet with them once a week and teach them management skills, such as how to calculate profit-and-loss, how to order products and supplies, how to run promotions, how to deal with customer relations, and how to structure operations for efficiency. We began meeting one hour every week on Tuesday during our slow time, around 3:00 in the afternoon. They gave themselves a nickname: MSG, the Management Support Group.

After that, the whole mood of the restaurant electrified. More hourly employees bought into my direction and ideas. They came to me and asked, "How can I be part of the MSG?"

Soon the original three assistant managers were standing together scratching their heads, whispering among themselves, until they came to me and said something like, "We're supposed to be managers, but we're not in charge of anything anymore."

"That's not true, you guys have keys and can open and close the restaurant each day. Listen, I'm the general manager, and my job is to give you direction, but you either refuse to do anything I ask or you flat-out ignore me. So rather than fight you, I found somebody who'll do what you won't. As it stands now, my hope is there'll be a day that you guys go somewhere else and I can manage this store with these other employees who actually want to work."

One by one, those managers came back to me and said, "Okay, I see what you're doing. I want to apologize and ask if I can get in on this." For a moment, I felt tempted to tell them they had their chance, but I found myself thinking about all the people who had given me second chances. Without them, I would never have made it this far. How could I not give these guys another shot? So, I gave them more responsibilities. But ultimately it was the kids who started the MSG who ran with it, young people with the vision to grasp an opportunity the moment they saw it.

I shared with the MSG the most important thing I had learned, that good management is not as much about what I do or how much faith I have in myself, as it is about what I can motivate others to do and how much faith I put in them. I gave my employees a sense of ownership, an opportunity to grow, and the support of a team. I didn't just march in and tell them what to do but instead offered them leadership training. In response, they rose to the occasion. I had learned this from the managers who had inspired me, who had seen my potential back when I was a shiftless screw-up who didn't know what I wanted. Their faith in me inspired me to step up. Now I did what my mother had taught me to do with that sort of generosity: I passed it on.

I knew morale was important, so I also created an atmosphere where people felt comfortable to cut loose a little, but without head-butting a toaster. One day I spotted our dishwasher's bike parked along the kitchen's back wall.

On a whim, I said, "Mind if I borrow your bike, Marcos? I'll be right back."

"Sure, boss."

I pulled the bike off the wall and climbed on, while everyone crowded into the kitchen to ask, "What're you doing?"

I rode the bike out of the kitchen and into the dining room, ringing the little bell on the handlebars, ding-ding-ding, as I pedaled past all the customers, around the bar, and back to the kitchen. Everyone was laughing. This was not a publicity stunt to build sales or marketing or anything like that. Sometimes you've just got to laugh. On the other hand, my little bike ride did make it into the local paper. Who knows? Maybe it was good marketing too.

A manager sets the tone for everything and everyone he manages. I was determined to set a tone of service to customers and success for employees. As a result, we not only gained customers, but all my original MSG team went on to become general managers and district managers. The three assistant managers who had undermined me never did catch on to the idea that giving is the key to receiving. Their careers continued to flounder, and I lost track of them.

During that first year, I sometimes returned to that speech my mom had asked me give in middle school, *Run to Win*. That's what I was doing. At each new challenge, I asked myself, "What do I think the limit is on what I can do?" Then I ran hard in hopes of surpassing that limit. The motivation for every step came from a vision of where I wanted to go, the outcome.

Where did I want to go? The bottom-line answer was: all the way.

***

Even though I had buy-in from the employees below me, that was impossible to achieve with one of the bosses above me. I had the support of my district manager, because he saw that I performed. But his boss was not a fan of my way. Kevin, the operations director, was a "we've always done it this way" kind of guy. The day Kevin saw my new host stand and my other changes to our procedures, he was pretty perturbed. I felt sure he would change his tune and congratulate me once he saw how dramatically I had decreased wait times and increased sales.

Instead he complained, "You know what, Keith? I don't think this is good. This isn't our standard. It's not the way we do things in this franchise group."

I tried to be polite, but I've never been good at hiding my irritation from people who make it their business to act like jerks just because they have a little power. "You want me to go back to crayons and no system?" I asked. "The new host stand and the rotation system work. We're proving it nightly. Why would I go back to a system that doesn't work?"

Here's why our system worked:

Applebee's did not take reservations, so the moment we were full, we started the wait. There were three main things I understood about a wait list: 1) quoting accurate wait times is important because you neither want to give customers false hope about a short wait only to tick them off if they wait too long, nor give them overly conservative estimates that make them give up on waiting in the first place; 2) pre-bussing tables while customers are still finishing up reduces the amount of time it takes to bus, saving up to thirty seconds per table on turn time, which can save many minutes per night on wait time, which means turning more tables overall; 3) knowing turn times helps improve accurate quotes on wait times. All of this means more profit.

Putting a manager at the host stand tied the whole system together. The manager was on top of the entire dining room dance. During busy times, the manager and host worked as a tag team to keep everything rotating smoothly. While the manager greeted guests, the host walked the floor to get updates on server stations. This helped us stay on top of rotating seating from station to station so no one server got slammed, which could slow down the turn times for that station because the server wouldn't be able to catch up.

The new system set a new tone for the restaurant. It made a difference for customers to see a professionally dressed manager out front instead of a uniformed teen with a crayon. The moment customers walked in, they received the impression that there were knowledgeable and accountable people in charge, which gave them more trust they'd be taken care of, which made them more relaxed, which led to a better experience, which made them more likely to return.

As a manager, I also understood that if we set in motion a good first turn of the dining room, that would set up our kitchen for a smooth flow of food orders for the rest of the night. At dinner, if we fell behind on that first turn, it would throw us off all night. But if we cleared that first turn with good service times, it set us up for happy customer experiences. The host stand was the hub that set that smooth flow going, so from the moment our guests came in until the moment they left, they would win and so would we. As manager, it was up to me to set an energetic attitude in motion, motivating everyone to maintain the rhythm that would keep everything flowing, similar to the way a drummer sets the beat for a band.

Not all my innovations were as big a success as the host stand. Our sales were so low when I first arrived, I knew that to prove myself, I needed to not only improve efficiency but also find creative ways to bring in more customers. So, I introduced "call-ahead seating" for lunch only. Customers could call in an order in advance, and we would reserve a table for them. When they arrived, the kitchen would already be making their order so that it would quickly arrive at the table. On slower days, this was a successful approach. On busier days, it was a mess.

You can bet, Kevin did his best to make me feel like a failure after that one. I didn't see it that way. The innovation had its merits. It simply didn't flow as well as I'd hoped. We had to drop that option, but I learned from my mistakes and continued to use the lessons learned to improve our approach to customer convenience.

As I shepherded that restaurant's rise from chaos to order, here's what I learned: being a good manager, or any kind of leader, requires organizational skills that connect small details to the big picture. More importantly, I discovered how to inspire people to take care of those small details by giving them a stake in the big picture.

By the end of my first year, I turned our store around from the single lowest sales compensation percentage to the highest in the company, meaning our staff made us way more money than they cost us. My people were the most productive in all of Applebee's. For that, I won the Applebee's Executive Award.

Although Kevin continued to naysay my innovations, the franchise owners came to meet me. They had heard of our runaway success and wanted to know how I managed it. They were most interested in my host stand program. After watching us in action, they said, "We want all of our stores to run the floor like this." Soon corporate sent somebody over to learn our hosting format and duplicate it as standard policy. Anybody who goes to an Applebee's today will see my host stand process still in action.

***

After only one year as general manager, I got promoted to district manager. That meant I oversaw six restaurants instead of one, and I had to up my ante at game-changing innovation. For my next big move, I took on an industry-wide problem: liquor inventory. We were losing money on booze, a perennial issue for restaurants. I knew from experience that if I wanted to change employee behavior, it didn't help to make angry accusations or give motivational speeches. To change behavior, I needed to focus not on tracking down the perpetrators but on having bartenders track the numbers. To do that, I switched my stores to a new inventory system called *sensitive inventory*.

Put simply, we required bar managers to fill out a form at end-of-shift, detailing how many units of each liquor item they had in the cooler from the previous shift, how much they added from the inventory in back, how much was left in the cooler at end-of-shift, and how many units they had sold. So, if we had nine bottles of Miller Lite from the previous shift in the front cooler, then pulled three Miller Lites from inventory, that would equal twelve units. Then if that bartender sold six units during shift, there should be six units left. If there were only five, the bartender would report a variance of one. Then the bartender for the next shift would start the process over again with the numbers from the previous shift.

If a bottle went missing one night, it might be a fluke, but if it happened to one bartender over and over, we would know that bartender was either drinking free beers or giving them away. That never happened. Once I created the new system, alcohol stopped disappearing. No bartender wanted to get caught with a variance column that said anything but zero. Zero meant they did their job that night. Zero every night meant they kept their job. Zero meant they stayed in the running for advancement. That's how we plugged the leaks in our alcohol inventory.

The sensitive inventory method proved what I already knew: if I wanted to change behavior, I had to focus not on the behavior but on the numbers. If I had admonished a bunch of bartenders, "Quit stealing from me!" they would have all nodded respectfully but not much would have changed. Instead, I said, "You're each re-sponsible for documenting your numbers," and whoever was steal-ing had to stop before the paperwork revealed them. I didn't have to ask them to tattle on each other, because the numbers took care of that. I didn't have to police them because the paperwork did it for me.

With that leak plugged, I put my energy into ideas that gave the bartenders the opportunity to use their creativity to increase sales. I did things like asking the bartenders to each create a new drink recipe and then compete to see whose drink yielded the highest sales. The winner received a $25 gift card. So instead of bartenders giving away free beer they were contributing to the bar's success, having fun, and giving themselves an opportunity to demonstrate their leadership and improve their chances for promotion.

The bars in all six of my restaurants stopped losing money and started seeing profit.

***

My successes did not rid me of the short-sighted, mean-spirited operations director, Kevin, who was now my direct supervisor. He continued to be a naysayer to all my innovations.

"Why do you always have to bootleg these ideas?" Kevin would say.

"I'm so tired of you calling me a bootlegger," I'd reply, and then explain in vain how the proof was in the numbers.

It seemed more important to Kevin to prove his underlings wrong than to motivate them to succeed. It probably didn't help that he had no knack for offering innovations of his own. All he could see was that my ideas made his lack of them look bad.

Despite Kevin, I did find a mentor in the front office. Archie was an operating partner who oversaw the entire Chicago market plus part of Florida. Archie was a guy's guy. He had the feel of a tough customer from a rough South Boston neighborhood. He'd been a football player, and even though he was 50 he could still bench-press 400 pounds. What I did for my restaurants, he did for our whole market: came into a franchise chain in disarray and brought back order. He had more experience than I did, and understood something I didn't yet: that the key to control was calm. Wherever there was chaos, Archie always brought calm.

Archie saw Kevin for what he was, a divide-and-conquer manipulator who undermined people's self-confidence and pitted colleagues against each other. Kevin saw the corporate ladder as something narrow you could only climb if you pulled down the person above you and stomped the hands of the person below you. He belittled people in front of their colleagues, and after he ran them off, laughed at them for being weaklings who couldn't take it.

Kevin was in charge of all of us district managers. He always identified someone he considered weak and made that person his target for torment. He made one guy provide a schedule on an hour-by-hour basis, listing each store he planned to visit each day, everything he planned to do there, and what time he planned to travel to the next location. Then Kevin would call him at random times and say, "Where are you?" If he was still at Location A when he was supposed to be at Location B, Kevin would write him up. We all knew about this because he called him out on it during our district meetings at the warehouse. He berated the young DM for failing to maintain a level of accountability that nobody could have lived up to.

After that guy gave up trying to please him and quit, Kevin moved on to his next target, one of the nicest guys I've ever met. Toby was a family man who loved to talk about his kids, an outgoing manager who was friendly with everyone, one of those guys who make people happy just to be around them. Meeting after meeting, Kevin laid into him: "I was in your store and I was appalled..." He'd go on to list the tiniest infractions—not poor customer service, dirty kitchens, or unsafe conditions, but things like one dusty rail, one missing light bulb, or a temporary shortage of shot glasses. Kevin always pointed out these failings with a smirk on his face. After maybe half a dozen meetings like that, Kevin had reduced Toby to a shell of a man, slumped in defeated silence.

Archie jumped in, "All right, Kevin, enough's enough."

Toby thanked Archie for standing up for him, but it was too late. He quit. Then Kevin moved on to his next target, and his next, until he got around to me.

Before he got halfway through his first complaints about my refusal to go by the book, I let out a snort. "You're so predictable. Ran out of weaklings to pick on, huh? Well, you're mistaken if you think you can scare me off."

He looked stunned. "Who do you think you're talking to?"

"I'm not sure, Kevin. Who do *you* think you are? You know, you can go into any restaurant in town this minute and list fifty things that are wrong. What you're doing has nothing to do with making our stores better. You're just running people off. Look at the graveyard of people behind you and look how many people you put there. This is not cool."

"This isn't about me, Keith, it's about you."

"Excuse me, if I'm going to have to sit through more of this I need to use the head first."

I walked out of the conference room, and actually went to the bathroom.

Kevin followed me and stood right outside the bathroom door. "Get out here!"

I took my time, but I finally had to step out. "Are you kidding me? Can't a guy go to the toilet without you wanting a detailed report?"

He got in my face, pointed at the conference room, and shouted, "You understand that man in there does not think you respect me? You have to respect me!"

"If you have to tell me to respect you, I don't think I'm the problem," I said.

He stepped up, leaned into my face, and put both hands on my chest. "You don't—"

Before he finished, I said through clenched teeth, "You need to get off me."

That's when Archie strode into the hall and came unglued. "What the hell are you guys doing out here?! This is my meeting!"

Although I respected Archie, I didn't back down. "Sir, I'm sorry, but this guy followed me to the bathroom, then he put his hands on me. I have a right to defend myself."

"Okay, okay. I understand you're upset, kid, but let's go back inside and work this out."

The look on Kevin's face said he knew Archie liked me better than him, and that was just another reason for him to hate me. But I refused to cower.

Archie phoned me the next night and said, "Hey, don't drag your tail in the dirt. I don't want you to get bothered about yesterday. You stand your ground the way you think you need to. I'll let you know if you're doing it wrong. But you've got to understand, Kevin is your boss."

I said, "Well, you've got to understand, he—"

"—No, I do understand. I just want you to know you're doing a great job. You know I think the world of you."

Not long after that, my son was born, and Archie mailed me a handwritten letter.

Dear Keith,
You're a great leader and you'll have a great career, but more important than that, you're going to be a great father.
Sincerely,
Archie Iodice

I framed that letter and it sits in my office to this day.

Archie finished teaching me the lessons my mom and dad had begun. Maybe his greatest lesson was to make me see things the opposite way Kevin did. I never competed against people working with me, no matter their place on the ladder. I came back to the lessons of distance running, which had taught me never to worry about those to my left or right, ahead or behind, but to focus on one competitor alone. There was only one person I always strove to outdo: myself.

As for Kevin, over time Archie helped me understand something about people like him. He knew Kevin was a poor leader, but he also knew management couldn't let him go without plenty of paperwork to back them up because he was the type who would fight. The day I quit the company, I listed among my reasons Kevin's history of cruel management tactics. The day I left, upper management let him go. They told me losing a leader like me made them realize this misguided manager was costing them too much.

He wasn't the only reason I left. I'd been at Applebee's six years and I was ready to move on, especially after my mentor, Archie, died of cancer. During my time in Chicago, my father, Ernie, Walter Payton, and Archie had all taught me what it takes to be a man of respect. They taught me that first I must learn to respect myself, then learn to help others experience that value in themselves.

With those lessons under my belt, I was ready to move on to a place where I could run to win on my own terms.

CHAPTER TWELVE

"DAD, ARE YOU COMING?"

Two are better than one, Because they have a good reward for their labor. For if they fall, one will lift up his companion. But woe to him who is alone when he falls, For he has no one to help him up. – Ecclesiastes 4:9-10

At first, fatherhood felt like another sort of second chance. Zachary was born in 2000, and I could not get over his simple existence. That's my boy, I thought, my chance to be the dad I once had, who never came all the way back though he tried. I wanted to pass down to him everything my dad had taught me: how to hunt and fish, the joy of throwing a ball, the rewards of hard work. I wanted to teach him what I had learned for myself: the thrill of running to win.

Zach was a typical little kid, and by that I mean he was perfect, with a smile and a sense of fun that brought back the boy I once was. We made snow angels in our yard in Chicago. We made a snowman and talked to him like he was a person. My favorite thing was to come home from work, take Zach's hand, and go for a walk. Not far, just down the sidewalk and back to the house, but he squealed when he saw me coming as if I were taking him to an amusement park. We loved being together.

"What'd you do today, Zach?"

"Mom let me ride my trike on the sidewalk. What'd you do?"

"My boss let me drive my car all over the city."

Zach would giggle and that would make me laugh in a carefree way I'd forgotten.

Sophie was born in 2002, almost exactly two years later. I adored her too, but I knew when I saw her that I wanted to protect her and wasn't sure I knew how. Annette was the only female I felt I had an understanding with. I had a feeling this new girl was going to put me through my paces. One kid felt like a new beginning, two felt like a weighty responsibility. If I wanted to make my big move, it had to be soon, before middle age and complacency set in, before I got into a routine and lost my hunger for more, before these kids needed money for college.

I put feelers out for new opportunities.

My goal was to own my own business, but I figured that was a ways off. I wasn't ready to search for investors or approach a bank and convince them to get behind a thirty-something guy with no college degree. But I knew I had talent, and I needed to get a move on into upper management, where I could make some seed capital and make a name for myself. So, I bought a new house in Chicago to make room for my growing family, and I interviewed with another Chicago chain.

That job didn't pan out, but a recruiter heard I was looking, called me up, and said he'd love to help me find the right position. He was motivated: the higher-level slot he could find for me, the bigger his commission, and he had heard my reputation was gold. His enthusiasm infected me, to the point that I gave in to an urge that had been gnawing at me. I was sick of Chicago winters and feeling homesick for Texas. I was ready to go home. I asked the recruiter to look for something in the Houston area.

One day he called me. "Hey, Keith, what do you know about Panera Bread?"

"I know them well. There's a bunch of them in Chicago."

"Well, there's none in Houston. Not yet. That's where you come in. I've got a new Panera franchisee who lives in Austin, but he wants to open a bunch of restaurants in Houston, and fast. He has absolutely no restaurant experience. He's looking for somebody to do it all."

"Do it all?"

"He'd make you a partner."

This guy would be a silent partner. He'd provide the money, I'd provide the sweat equity. If I got the position, I could work my way into ownership without coughing up capital. If.

The way it worked with Panera, both the franchise and the local franchisee had to sign off on me as a partner. I talked to the franchisee, Mark, on the phone. I was still a district manager for Applebee's, and shortly after my call with Mark one of the guys from Panera's franchise operations stopped by one of my restaurants to see me in action. He waited till I finished talking to the general manager, then called me over to where he sat at the bar.

He pointed at me. "Keith, you're our guy."

"I appreciate that, but that's kind of Mark's decision I would think."

"No, you're our guy." He gave me the kind of grin that said the decision was made.

He and another corporate head sat with Mark, and he later said they told him the same thing, in no uncertain terms: "Keith is your operating partner. He knows his stuff."

They immediately extended an offer to me. Based on their faith in me, Mark offered to vest me in the operations from the start. I knew that was unusual.

Most operating partners have to wait at least a couple of years before they receive a percentage of profits from the business. The idea is to protect the investing partners, to give them time to make sure they've found a good fit. Nobody wants to hand off a percentage of their business to somebody, only to find out that person is not who you think he is. On the other hand, this can be scary for the operating partner, who might put in thousands of hours setting up new operations and making them profitable, right until it's time for him to vest, only for the franchisees to fire him and bring in somebody they don't have to pay any vesting. I recognized the trust my new partner was giving me from the start, based on my reputation and the intuition of the guy from Panera who had watched me deal with people for only an hour.

I had not expected things to move so fast, to become a business owner and find my way home to Houston all at once, but this was my chance to build something from scratch. I never even considered turning it down.

Annette and I had moved into a new house two months earlier, and now we would have to move again. We were both stressed, and if she was more stressed than me, I was too overwhelmed to notice. She had been understanding about the pull of home for me, and had supported my job search, but I think the reality put her in mild shock. She had grown up in Chicago, never lived anywhere else.

Annette had quit teaching to be a stay-at-home mom while the kids were small. I told her this made it a perfect time to move. If we waited until the kids started school and she went back to work, a move would be harder. She conceded that. I told her we could say goodbye to freezing winters. She liked that. I told her this partnership was a great opportunity for our future as a family. That convinced her. Still, she cried a lot, especially the day she hugged her parents goodbye.

I put an arm around her as we drove away, told her so long as we were together it would be okay. "We're a family," she agreed. "We're in this together."

***

There was no time to settle in, visit old friends, or get reacquainted with home. The day I arrived in Houston, I met with my new partner, Mark. He was only a few years older than me, and if possible, even more ambitious. He had created an aggressive schedule: to open four new Paneras in a year. We didn't have any properties yet. My primary job would be to find the real estate, build the franchises, hire and train the employees, and stock the restaurants. I had never bought commercial property or managed a construction project. I had hired and trained people before, but never this many. As if all that didn't make me nervous enough, Mark was having trouble explaining what he wanted, other than four new Paneras in a year.

"Do you have a project manager?" I asked.

He shook his head. "We've got you."

"Do you have a training handbook?"

"No, I've got you."

"What about your other partner?"

"He's a lawyer. This isn't really his area."

"You've got me."

He nodded. "Now you're getting it. Can you do it?"

I had no idea, but I said, "I'm your guy."

Once I said that, I knew I would stand by it, because I'm a man of my word. So what if I didn't know what I was doing yet? I'd learn. I knew how to run to win, and I was about to test my new limit for how fast I could move and how far I could go. Anything I didn't understand about contracts, I would have our other partner look at. He was a lawyer. For everything else, I'd keep running till I hit a wall, then I'd hire someone to tear down the wall, and run some more.

Mark drove back to Austin and left everything to me.

I wanted to come home and assure my wife this was the best move I'd ever made. Instead I felt numb that night as I told Annette, "I'm not sure I've done my homework here. I've moved our family from Chicago to Houston, we've got two kids to feed, I'm in charge of a startup with two partners who know nothing about restaurants, and the guy in charge lives three hours away."

"You'll figure it out, Keith," she said. "That's why they picked you. You're good at that."

It helped that she believed in me. It didn't occur to me she might need someone to root for her too. I was too overwhelmed to see beyond the next task, and the next, one after another. The freedom to run my own show was exhilarating, but I was in over my head, wearing all the hats. Our company was called Rolling Dough, but in my head I named it Keith Against The World. That idea of myself as a superhero helped on hard days, which was pretty much every day for the next three years.

I made mistakes. My first one was choosing the wrong real estate for one of our restaurants. A broker drove me around Houston and pointed at spots left and right. One site had a few red flags, but I rationalized them away. We were already behind, so I was in a hurry to start building. The location did not look inviting for customers, but I decided it had enough traffic flow to make up for that. I figured even if we had low volume, the rent structure was cheaper than other options, so we could make up money there. I learned the hard way to never decide that doing less in sales can be profitable. My first instinct had been right; the rent structure was so low because it was a terrible site. We had to close that store within a few months of opening.

The lessons came hard, but they've served me since: Trust my instincts, don't rationalize, and never buy anything I have to talk myself into.

Once I felt my way through buying properties, I moved on to the next thing I didn't know how to do: running multiple building projects in one year. I spent a lot of hours walking around construction sites, kicking boxes and boards in frustration because I didn't know what I was doing. This was the definition of on-the-job training. But I kept learning.

Then I started hiring. Since we didn't have an employee handbook, I wrote one. Not from scratch. I grabbed a couple of handbooks from places I had worked and modeled ours after their most useful sections. Every document we used in our operations from then on, I put together.

I had never been responsible for bringing a new brand into a market. This required me to suss out the competition, local sandwich shops that were long established. My job was to cut away a slice of their market share, or preferably—since I prefer to be a hero, not a villain—carve out a whole new market. Nobody in Houston knew who Panera was. Not then. I was a guy in my thirties, so I portrayed myself and this enterprise as the young, energetic underdog. Because I ran a franchise, it was easy to surround myself with young, gung-ho people like me who could help sell that image. Our greatest asset was that we were "young, new, and fresh." So that was the message we pushed in all our marketing.

After the first year, our third partner dropped out, and it was just Mark and me. Luckily, that relationship worked great. He'd tell me what he wanted, and I would execute. The good news was, I was on my own. The bad news was, I was on my own.

I continued to make so many mistakes my goal became: just don't make the same mistake twice. But I never saw them as failures, always as learning experiences I could build on. If I had to do it again, I might have slowed down our ramp-up: start one store, get it going, and make sure it's a win before opening the next. I learned the win is not just the brand. The win is the location, the demographics of the clientele, the relationships we build with the community.

Mark relying so heavily on me allowed me to grow faster in my career. I rose to the occasion. Annette was right, that's why they picked me. Whatever I tried, I was all in. Like they say in baseball, I was determined to be either the hero or the goat. Right or wrong, whatever I did, I liked it best when the ball was in my hand.

I opened seven restaurants in five years. I took no vacations. I rarely took a day off. All our restaurants took off, except that one dud location, and I caught that mistake early enough to sell it and cut our losses. Soon our bottom line started to rise, with Rolling Dough poised to do just what its name promised and roll us in dough.

But although my dedication paid off for my business, it did no favors for my marriage. Annette was home alone with our kids at our new house in Humble, a small suburb outside Houston. I hardly saw my family anymore.

***

I had left Texas a dozen years before to shake an obsession with drugs, alcohol, and living like there was no tomorrow. I used to miss a lot of work because I was amped up on coke, or exhausted from being amped up on coke. Now it was as if work had become the little white line that kept me buzzing like a live wire. My family faded into the dull background. Sophie was so little, I didn't think she was missing much by me not being there. And Zach was still too young for big conversations. I figured this was the perfect time for me to pay my dues at work and I would catch up with my kids soon enough.

I didn't realize Annette had become a stranger to me until it was too late. I had such tunnel vision about work, I didn't notice any empty places inside me. I had no time to ask myself simple questions like: "Do I miss my wife?" or "Wouldn't it be nice to play with the kids?" When people talked about being married to a career, I got what they meant, not because I knew I had my priorities backward, but because that's how it *felt*: like my career was the life partner who satisfied my every need, like I could live without companionship, sex, or kids, because I was in love with the high of success.

Work became my religion. My workplace became the space where I formed and nurtured relationships, and those relationships felt vital. I was giving young people work, mentoring future leaders, feeding people, serving the public. All while providing security for my family. What higher purpose could there be? If there were a God, surely even He would approve. But I wasn't thinking about God. I was just doing what I do best: solving problems, making things happen, connecting with everyone. Everyone, that is, except my wife.

All I could think about were things like: I've got this deadline,

I've got to make these hires, I have to sign these contracts, I have to make these orders, I have to close on this real estate deal. There was too much to do for me to stop and ask myself, "How are you feeling, Keith? How's your family? How's your life? How are you?"

I'd heard of the term *workaholic*, but it always sounded like a backhanded brag, one of those obsessions Americans pretend is bad for them even though they're secretly proud of it.

I didn't understand I was in the throes of another addiction until it was too late.

Annette and I didn't fight. In fact, we didn't talk much at all. How could she connect with somebody who was not there? After the first two years, a night came when I slept in the spare room so I wouldn't wake her. The next night, she asked me to keep sleeping there—so I wouldn't wake her.

The moment was awkward, like a conversation with an irritable roommate. I said something like, "This isn't working."

To which she said something like, "No, it isn't."

After a few weeks or months of sleeping in the spare room, I said, "I'm moving out."

"Okay," she said, and that was that.

I moved to an apartment in the city.

The biggest surprise was how little we had to say about what should have felt like a major change, but didn't. I felt disconnected from our life together, like someone had pulled a plug. I didn't feel all that much the day I left. As for Annette, she just looked tired of it all. If she felt more than that, she wasn't telling me. We had forgotten how to talk to each other.

The next time we talked, I said, "Why don't we just divorce?" I had once thought divorce was the single worst choice two people could make. Now it felt like the next logical step.

Annette agreed to that, too. The conversation lasted maybe two minutes.

I went online and researched "do-it-yourself divorce" to avoid wasting time, money, and emotion on attorneys and courtrooms. I was happy to give Annette whatever she wanted. I knew she was a good wife and mother. I didn't believe it was her fault, or mine, that we drifted apart.

After a few weeks at my apartment, one day I drove to the house in Humble to pick up Zach and Sophie for a Sunday visit, and then dropped them back off as usual. Sophie was two, and she didn't act like she noticed anything out of the ordinary about our new living situation. After all, we had told the kids many times that Dad worked a lot. Now Dad was just working more. Sophie accepted that and let her mom take her inside the house without a second glance at me.

But Zach was four, old enough to know I was leaving to go back to my new apartment downtown. He knew my apartment was not home. This house was home, and he knew daddies and mommies live at home. He knew this wasn't normal. I hugged him goodbye and turned down the walkway toward my car.

Zach ran after me. "Dad, are you coming? Why aren't you coming?"

He wasn't at the stage where I could sit him down and say, hey, let me explain why parents get divorced and how none of it's your fault. I think I told him, "Zach, it's gonna be okay. Mom's here. It's gonna be okay. I'll see you in a couple of days. I'll call you tonight."

That wasn't enough for Zach. He cried—hard. "Why aren't you coming?" His big wet eyes looked too much like mine, and all I could think was: *He's so little.*

All he wanted was to have his whole family together again. All he wanted was for me to come in. There was no way to explain why I couldn't.

I walked away, got in the car, and cried all the way back to Houston.

CHAPTER THIRTEEN

A Husband and Father

I left the lights off when I entered my apartment. The place didn't seem much different than it did when I turned them on. It had the nondescript furniture of a place that is no home, just somewhere to sleep. I sat on the uncomfortable couch that came with the furnished apartment, put my head in my hands, and continued to cry, big ugly sobs that would have embarrassed me if there were anybody around to witness them. I couldn't help thinking I deserved to feel like this because I had made my little boy cry. I felt alone. Worse, I felt ashamed. I feared that, despite all my second chances, I had turned into a bad man, the opposite of what my parents had raised me to be. This was not something that had happened to me. It was something I had done.

I still believed that whatever brought Annette and me together was dead, but I knew I was the one who had killed it. One question remained: Would a good man try to revive a dead relationship for the sake of his kids?

There were no secrets in my family. My father, big sister, brother, aunts, uncles, and cousins, had all poured one idea into my ear since word got around that Annette and I had separated: "Marriage is tough, but you have to work through those tough times." I had thought they didn't understand, but was I the one who failed to understand? Was I giving up too easily? Was I being selfish? What other explanation was there for me walking away from my son when he begged me to stay because he wanted his daddy?

I called into the dark, "What the hell did I do to my kids?" For the first time in years, I spoke as if God were listening. For the first time in years, I half-expected an answer.

I had told myself when Zachary was born it was going to be important to raise him in a Godly way. Not because I was a believer. I had continued to doubt God was anything more than a comforting fiction people dreamed up to make sense of life and death. Despite that, I yearned for my son to grow up with the faith that made my childhood happy, at least until my mom died. I didn't want Zach to experience church as a chore, or the Bible as no more than an instruction manual for right and wrong. I wanted him to get the idea he was on this earth for a reason, that someone or something loving watched out for him, that hard work and kindness mattered.

I wanted to give him something greater to believe in than Santa Claus, the Easter Bunny, and the Tooth Fairy.

Once I had cracked open that door, it was hard to close it. I had come to hope God existed as something more than a fairytale to keep people in line. Annette came from a strong Christian family, and I'd known better than to tell them I was an atheist. Sometimes, watching her parents hold hands, bow their heads, and pray together over a meal or a problem got me thinking of my parents, though they were very different people. It was hard to see the fault in something that clearly brought these people closer together. Over the years, I started questioning: is this all phony, or is there a God after all?

Still, if any adult outside the family ever asked me, "Are you a Christian?" my honest answer remained, "No."

By the time we moved to Houston, Zach was old enough to have an idea what church was, and it didn't seem right to tell him to go if I didn't go too. Besides, my son's natural curiosity about God, Jesus, the prophets, and all their stories got me curious about what all those things might mean to me now. So, our whole family started going to church. I didn't experience a spiritual awakening, but I did enjoy the services. They reminded me of my mom, but no longer in a sad way, in a good way, like even if I didn't find God, I was finding my mother again somewhere in the hymns and scriptures she once loved.

But now, sitting alone crying on this rented apartment couch, I got to thinking about my mom again, and it didn't feel so good. I thought how I used to have two perfect parents, and how when my mom died I lost them both. I'd had no choice: my mom died, and my dad was destroyed. But my children had two healthy parents, and I was depriving them of the opportunity to experience a complete family. I thought of how I felt when my original family shattered, how angry I was at God, how I walked so far from them and Him that I ended up alone in a jail cell. Now here I was again, alone, and this time the cell was dark.

By this point, Annette had moved into a tiny house, a single-mom kind of house that didn't have room for me anymore. I imagined another man might soon be tucking Zach and Sophie into bed each night, all because I'd taken the easy way out. Did that mean I wanted to stay married to Annette? I didn't know. Even if I did, I'd drifted so far away, there was no telling if she wanted to be married to me anymore. It was not as if she had put up a fight when I left. She'd just accepted it, like the weather.

I dried my eyes, went to bed, and next morning I went back to work. No matter my regrets, I figured it was too late to change course now.

Not long after my night alone in the dark, I got a call from one of my cousins on my mother's side. Bart was a man of faith who had joined the ministry. Once upon a time I would have told Bart to peddle his religious garbage somewhere else, but what with my late-night cry and unplanned plea for an answer from God, I wondered if this was His way of answering—through my mom. Or as close to her as I was going to get in this life. God was still not high on my priority list, but since I'd called on Him on the off chance He was listening, it might be rude to hang up on His possible messenger. Whatever Bart said during that call went in one ear and out the other, though no doubt he mentioned something about the sanctity of marriage and how this was not about me but about something bigger than me.

Then Bart mailed me a book. I didn't read it.

Next time he called, I still didn't hang up, but I still didn't listen all that well either. He asked if I had read the book he sent. "I'm not really a book guy," I said. "You got something with pictures, I'm your guy."

He laughed, and started sending me handwritten letters. They might as well have been a book; those letters were each ten to twenty pages long, filled with tiny writing. By then, I was desperate for answers, so I read them all. Next time he called, I asked a bunch of follow-up questions about what he'd written. Once I opened that door wider, he began calling me regularly to counsel me and pray with me. If he had only talked about faith, he might have lost me, but he focused on family as a vehicle for faith. Our moms were sisters, and they had always been deep-rooted in the principles of God first, family and everything else second. Bart talked about how putting family first is one expression of putting God first.

He caught my full attention when he talked about what I owed my kids. "Your children are learning about marriage by watching you," he said. It took me longer to accept what he had to say about what I owed my wife, like this quote from Ephesians 5:25: "Husbands, love your wives, just as Christ also loved the church and gave Himself for her."

The more Bart and I talked, the more I felt like God had sent him as a messenger, and the more I felt God reaching out to me through that messenger, the more I realized how far I had retreated from God. Instead of comforting me, this made me feel worse. The more I yearned to get close to God, the more depressed I felt. The more depressed I felt, the deeper I dove into isolation.

It got to the point that my days went like this: work seventeen hours, eat junk all day, go to my favorite neighborhood bar to toss back five drinks, pass out, then roll out of bed and start again. I became such a regular at one bar, they greeted me like Norm Peterson from *Cheers*: "Hey, Keith!" I discovered that if everyone at the bar knows your name, sometimes it's not so great. Sometimes it means you've hit rock bottom.

Getting up each morning got harder. Those first few moments after I woke, I would stare at the ceiling through bloodshot eyes and wonder, is this what the rest of my life is going to be?

***

Nine months into my separation from Annette, I was driving to my favorite bar from one of my half-dozen Panera restaurants with my car radio tuned to a country station, when a song caught my attention. I don't remember the name of the song, just a singer saying something like, "I'm not sure if where I'm going is better than where I've been."

"Ain't that the truth!" I told myself.

Here I was, a guy with a beautiful wife and two amazing kids, and I was headed to a shitty bar, so I could get shitty drunk, so I could stand spending another night alone in my shitty apartment. Somewhere in the middle of that self-pity, the question I had been avoiding came to me. Not, "What did I do to my kids?" or, "What did I do to myself?" but, "What did I do to my wife?"

I felt so sorry, and I wanted her to know that more than anything. The moment the remorse sank in, I missed her so much it felt like a punch in the gut. I knew then that I still loved her, though I could not understand how that was possible after I'd about starved our love to death. The question now was: Did she still love me?

Either that night or the next I called her up and asked, "Is there any way you would consider talking to me?"

"About what?"

"About working things out, maybe getting back together?"

"No," she said, and hung up.

I sat there, stunned, and thought, "Okay then. I asked. That's all I can do. Time to move on."

But I could not bring myself to move on until I was sure I had tried everything. I took Bart's advice and prayed, asked God to please open the door to my wife's heart. "If that's your will, Lord," I added, because it was clear I had lost control of this situation long ago. My indifference had done so much damage to Annette, to both of us, to all of us, that I needed a miracle to pull this family together.

While I waited on God's answer, I continued the routine of doing anything to avoid going home to my apartment. I probably should have done AA or some kind of recovery program, but I didn't. Days passed, maybe weeks, and nothing changed. I gave up. I never asked Annette again about getting back together.

She's the one who called me, one day out of the blue. "When you drop the kids off Sunday, why don't you stay and we can sit and talk."

I was stunned. My stomach churned all day Saturday. I don't remember what the kids and I did that day, but I'm sure I kept staring at them like I was obsessed. This had to work or our family would be destroyed.

The next day, Annette and I sat in her new kitchen to talk, another place that felt nothing like home. Every piece of familiar furniture squeezed into this unfamiliar place served as a reminder of my failure. The conversation was awkward, like we barely knew each other, like I was negotiating an arranged marriage with a stranger.

"Why do you want to get back together?" she asked.

I told her I still loved her, told her I didn't realize keeping a marriage alive took work, told her I knew I had failed to give my marriage the same commitment I'd given my career. I said that I wanted to be a father and a husband, that I missed being a family, that I knew I could not be the man I wanted to be without her and the kids.

After that, she did most of the talking. I was okay with that because I was the one who had disappeared, long before I physically left her. We each confessed our biggest beefs with the other, though none of it came as a revelation. She said I worked too much, didn't spend enough time with the kids, and disconnected myself from her. I said she spent too much money.

We shied away from using words like "demands," but Annette laid two non-negotiable items on the table: "You have to make time for the kids, and you have to be more available and communicate more with me."

It took several more visits for us to decide what all that meant. In the end, we came to an agreement, I got rid of the apartment, and moved Annette out of her tiny house. Together we moved into a bigger place and rearranged our individual lives, this time keeping each other, and our whole family, in mind every step of the way.

Once we reconciled, I stopped drinking. It wasn't that hard for me, because I had never really wanted to go someplace where everyone knew my name. I had simply wanted to go home.

To become a better father and husband, I realized I had to prioritize family time the way I prioritized work time. So, I came up with father-oriented tasks to accomplish, and scheduled them on my calendar, just like I did with work. Not because I saw my family as a series of tasks, but because organizing my life around responsibilities that would lead to success was something I knew how to do.

I became a baseball coach for Zach's Little League team, and I created daddy-daughter outings for Sophie and me: ice cream, lunch, playing in the park. Wednesday night became family night, when we'd all get together to go to dinner and do something fun. This was Annette's and my version of a date-night because we loved being together as a family.

I came to see there had always been, and would only ever be, one question I needed to answer about marriage and family: what was I willing to do to be as successful a father and husband as I was a restaurant-owner and entrepreneur? The specifics of my answer might change from day to day, but it always sprang from the same philosophy I applied to work: whatever I did I needed to go all the way, to be the hero or the goat. My parents had taught me the importance of both work and family. Their work ethic had stuck, and my new goal was to apply that same ethic to family.

It worked. Annette and I grew close again. If anything, she became more beautiful to me than ever, inside and out. Maybe I had needed to see how bleak life was without her to appreciate all she gave to our family.

It occurred to me maybe God had worked this miracle in answer to my prayers. Maybe He had nudged Annette to believe in me when she had no reason to trust I would deliver. I began to pray more intentionally, not just in church but on my own time. I still wasn't sure God listened. But I was also no longer sure He didn't. How could I give up the relationship that had helped bring my family together again? If it was a relationship with a fantasy, so be it. It worked.

The more I thanked God for my blessings, the more I saw marriage and fatherhood not as burdens but as rewards. I watched Zach hit his first grand slam and pitch his first no-hitter. I watched Sophie's volleyball games and dance recitals—which I'll admit was a little harder. Much as all the traditionally male activities were easier for me to understand, I was surprised to discover that Sophie was more of a driven, gregarious, overachiever like me, while Zach was more sensitive and quiet like his mom. And to watch both of them grow from children into productive adults who will someday have families of their own? How had I almost let myself miss that? The opportunity to lead my kids on the path to their own successes has turned out to be the greatest privilege of my life.

I used to think my mom and dad were perfect. Then my mother

died, and I saw my father reduced from superhero to mortal. Now I understood something I had failed to get back then: No family is perfect, but together they can become more than they are apart.

The truth is, Annette and I have not stuck hard and fast to our non-negotiables like we promised each other: I still work too much, and she still spends too much. But I also work hard at family, and when I'm with them I'm all in. I do everything that way, and Annette has come to appreciate that's just how I'm wired. Meanwhile, Annette tries to stay on a budget, and if she overspends she's more likely to do so in service to our family and community. I've come to appreciate that this is simply another side of her generous spirit, which is how she's wired.

The rest of it, we let go. That was our biggest lesson. My dad, my sister, brother, aunts, uncles, and cousin Bart were right. When marriage gets tough, that's not when it ends. That's when the hard work begins. Once Annette and I found that out and accepted it, that's when our marriage started to grow. Today it's not as much about what we're able to negotiate as what we're willing to understand, or if we can't understand, what we accept without judgment.

That wasn't the biggest test we would face, though. Not by a long shot. It was just the first big test, the one we needed to tell us that together we could weather whatever storms might come.

CHAPTER FOURTEEN

THE TEAM

A man will be as a hiding place from the wind, And a cover from the tempest, As rivers of water in a dry place, As the shadow of a great rock in a weary land. – Isaiah 32:1 - 2

Rolling Dough, Ltd. was a dicey proposition from the start. We did not open strong. We had no brand awareness, and this was not only because our customers were not familiar with Panera Bread, but also because we weren't either. Was it fast food? Yes, and no. A bakery or coffee shop? Yes, and no. A sandwich shop? Sort of, but more than that. The only opportunity to identify ourselves that we jumped on from the start was "casual catering." If a church wanted bagels, we showed up with bagels. If a school fundraiser needed lunch for their volunteers, we showed up with sandwiches. If a small business needed coffee and pastry for a meeting, we showed up with that too. We became a go-to option around the idea of *community.*

We did not have a budget for marketing on a community-wide level. We just got out there and served community events, and counted on word of mouth to get our name out there. We were betting on this as a long-term play. It was no small risk. We knew at first our costs would be high and our sales would be low.

I understood that this is the way things work when you're building initial trust with customers. The job is to make sure you have plenty of product and plenty of staff, keep putting yourself out there...and wait.

For five years, we collected debt. Entering 2008, I was nervous. I wrote a budget projecting that, if we continued as we were, we would be on track to lose a million dollars. I was ready to bail.

One night, Annette and I lay awake in bed talking into the wee hours.

"This is just not the right fit for me," I said.

She took my hand. "No. I think you need to keep doing this. You're good at solving big problems and coming up with big ideas. This isn't the moment to quit, this is the kind of moment you were made for." Annette had a way of dissolving my doubts—just like that.

"You're right. I've worked too hard to give up now."

I realized I'd picked the wrong emotional reaction. Instead of giving in to defeat, I got mad. And anger fueled me to make a bold plan.

I called a meeting with my partner, Mark. "Our biggest problem?" I said. "We have to come to terms with where we've failed: we've opened several bad locations."

"Well then," Mark said. "What are we going to do?"

"We need to close two of these crappy locations, maybe three—"

"That's almost a third of our operations!"

"I'm not finished... Then we need to open three more."

I can't remember what Mark said to that, but we both agreed there was no model out there that suggested my idea was anything other than nuts. When sales are slowing down, most people don't throw good money after bad and open more locations. But I felt we were still in the early growth phase and the bad locations were simply a detour along the way. In the early growth phase, you always spend more than you bring in. I convinced Mark we were at a stronger point in our development than it might seem, because we had learned a lot about the area. We both felt confident about two things: the locations I suggested selling were a drag on our profits, and the locations I suggested buying had sure-fire potential.

Maybe we were young and foolish, but one thing for sure: we both wanted to be the hero or the goat. We agreed that if we were going to make a go of this, we needed to go all the way.

The only reason we could afford this kind of risk was because Mark had a great relationship with the bank. Most banks would have asked, "Are you out of your mind?" Instead, Mark's bank said, "We trust you."

We negotiated to exit our deals with the landlords of the three dying stores. Then we opened three new ones. The moment we opened the doors to those three new locations, sales took off. With that move, we began reaching our target audience, which helped us better understand our target audience, who in turn began getting the message about what we were offering. We became the go-to lunch-meeting place for people on the go, which also increased our reputation as the go-to caterer for casual events.

The same year that we took this mighty risk, 2008, the stock market crashed. We held our breath, but Houston didn't take as big a hit as the rest of the country did during the Great Recession. The economic uncertainty of the time might even be what gave us a small boost, because our segment of the industry was fast-casual. Everybody was watching their nickels and dimes more than usual, and Panera was the perfect place for that.

Three years later we were doing so well, we opened up a chain of Carl's Juniors.

***

My favorite thing about my career is creating opportunities: op-portunities for employees to grow as leaders and provide for their families, opportunities for customers to feel immersed in hospi-tality, opportunities for families, friends, and colleagues to grow relationships. For me, restaurants are all about community.

Greg and Tina Garvey worked with me for years in Chicago, back when I was with Applebee's. I hired Greg as a manager and Tina as a bartender. They met on the job, dated, fell in love, got married, and became the kind of team that adds to that sense of camaraderie that makes a restaurant a special place to be. I was not the easiest manager back then, a perfectionist who had trou-ble managing my expectations, yet they still went above and be-yond for me, and remained gracious to a fault. Loyalty is maybe my most prized value, and they showed me the kind of loyalty I couldn't help but return.

When I left Chicago for Houston, they followed, and I was grateful to have them in my corner from the get-go. Whatever I asked, from "Hey, I need you to work late," to "I need you to not take a vacation for the first year," they were always ready with an enthusiastic, "No problem, Keith. Anything for you." Sometimes I needed to blow off steam, and they sat and listened to me, for hours, even when I told them, "You guys don't have to keep me company." They were not just employees, but friends in the truest sense.

I made Greg my facilities manager and put Tina in charge of catering. She was the main reason that was our strongest suit from the beginning.

For the rest of my hires, I flew by the seat of my pants. I didn't know a lot about hiring at first, so I started with the idea of trying to see prospective employees as a mirror, to see if any of my own best qualities reflected back. I was always looking for the underlying potential I could help bring out in them, the way my mentors had done for me. I did not want a bunch of mini-me's, just people with the kind of spark I could relate to.

One candidate, Jenny, had attended the University of Houston. She hadn't graduated, but she had worked in restaurants her whole life and she had a do-whatever-it-takes work ethic. The spark she had that grabbed my attention was her laugh. It rang with authenticity, it was contagious, and it was big. I remember imagining how that woman's God-given laugh would warm the environment of the restaurant. To me, her laughter embodied a whole culture, one I wanted to be part of. My instinct to hire that laughter was a good one. Jenny was with me for more than half a dozen years, and worked her way up to assistant manager before moving on. During that time, her laugh lit up our Pasadena Panera just like I thought it would.

That's the way it went with many leaders I hired, several of whom started as hourly employees but are regional managers today. They worked their way through the ranks like I did. A lot of restaurant chain owners operate at high altitude, propped in towers at 30,000 feet, and they see their business from that angle. Although I appreciate the importance of the bird's eye view, whenever I walk into my restaurants I always walk the line and shake the hands of every hourly employee. I never forget where I came from. I'm all for giving opportunities to those kids who don't have a long list of achievements, but who are eager for the chance to show what they're made of. I don't see myself as giving them opportunities so much as giving them a place to create their own opportunities.

A lot of people start in this business young, and young people often call for a combination of expectation and patience. The way I encourage young leaders is by giving them that little extra push, not pressure so much as a nudge in the right direction, toward more, toward better. I'm a patient man, but I never settle. I'm never content to sit still. When my people leap over a hurdle, I immediately want to clear the next one. That's the quality I seek in employees. In that way, I'm a kind of coach, always pushing my team to run their best race, to run to win.

Although I always want more, I don't want it as much for me as for those around me. I'm not only looking at how I can take things to the next level, but also how I can help others achieve their next level. I'm protective of my people: employees, friends, family. They're all my team.

***

We had maybe five days' warning about Hurricane Ike, but what we had no way of knowing was whether or not Houston would face a direct hit. Years of management had taught me that planning ahead offers an edge in any situation, so we planned what to do if this hurricane did not bounce west to Mexico or east to Florida, like they usually did. Thanks to my promise to become a more involved parent, I had helped Annette create a phone tree with other parents whose kids did activities with ours, to keep track of everyone's kids in case of emergency. I repurposed that idea to create a phone tree for our restaurants, so that during the hurricane we could keep track of where all our employees were and what their responsibilities were during the storm.

Word came down that the hurricane looked to hit Houston hard. The phone tree helped us roll everyone into immediate action on phase one of our hurricane plan: boarding up, shutting down, heading home, and packing their own stuff to head north.

I made the decision to stay in town and ride it out.

Ike was a Category 5 hurricane, at that time the biggest beast I had ever seen, with 180- to 200-mile-an-hour winds. Although the winds were scary, the flooding was worse.

My family was spared the worst of the storm, but our neighborhood lost power for ten days. The kids, Annette, and I stayed with her parents, who now lived in Houston. They lived in the same neighborhood we did, so the only reason we stayed in their house was for security in numbers. There were curfews, so nobody was supposed to be out after dark, but houses were getting looted. We slept with guns at hand.

It wasn't the end of the world. It just felt like it.

I remember being glad that at least I had one less thing to worry about because I had a hurricane plan for Panera. The moment the power came back, I set phase two of the plan into action. I sent word down the phone tree: "Let's open up our restaurants!" Problem was, we had lost power so long most of our perishable food had to be thrown away. I had managers working overtime to get food brought in, which called for logistical wizardry. Luckily, I had hired people who were up for a challenge and who understood the effectiveness of collective effort.

Every day I drove to our office to meet with our team leaders, six or seven of us. I clapped my hands together to signal I was game. "Here's what we're going to do…" I began with total confidence, even though I'd never before been through anything like this. But I was an experienced manager, and this was a situation that called for one. Everything I'd been through to this point had prepared me for this moment.

The key was that we had planned in advance how we would communicate, stay connected, and play our individual roles while also working as a team. Our community-minded approach helped us open within less than forty-eight hours of having power. Ike devastated many a restaurant in the Houston market, but we were up and running weeks before many of our competitors, serving a stunned community. We succeeded all because we ran that race as a team.

I knew then that, if there was a God, then He had given me a gift of leadership strong enough not only to weather storms, but also to help others find the strength to hold together through winds, floods, and darkness. It turned out this would be good to know.

CHAPTER FIFTEEN

UNCLE KEITH

A friend loves at all times, and a brother is born for a difficult time. – Proverbs 17:17

One thing still bewildered me: my brother, Kyle, had somehow reached his forties without finding his own path to leadership. My big brother—who used to beat me up when I was little, who tried to pull me back on track when I went off the rails, who held fast to his faith in God when I lost mine—was still struggling to find himself. He had always been the sensitive one in the family. He had suffered under our father's demands for hard work and excellence in ways I never understood, because even back then I thought Dad was simply teaching us good values. Most important, Kyle had never figured out how to transform his faith into his rock.

Even though he was an adult when my mother died, I'm not sure he ever recovered from the fracturing of our family.

He had a creative streak, and I suppose Dad never knew how to encourage that side of him. Kyle self-published a novel in 2000, when he was 32. *Music Makes Memories* was the story of ten Gen-X friends, a sort of lost-generation story that he admitted was based on his own life. I never read it, and that bummed him out. It wasn't that I had no interest in my brother. I'm just not a reader, never read a book in my life, not even the ones they assigned in school. The sad truth was Kyle's book didn't get much interest from anybody. He never sold more than a handful of copies.

So, Kyle gave up on his dream of becoming a bestselling author and went on to start his own business in Chicago, a bar called The Blue Monkey. To me, this seemed promising, an answer to the call of our father's entrepreneurial spirit, a call I had gladly answered. But The Blue Monkey floundered. Kyle tried a few other jobs and investments along the way, always grasping for some idea to launch his own success story, but he was all over the board. Restless. For a brief time, he tried selling produce for somebody, and I gave them an account at Panera. He worked hard, and the deal went well. But it didn't last—just another of his short-lived entrepreneurial schemes.

At one point, Kyle ended up back in Conroe, fell in love, and got married. He and his wife moved to Louisiana, where he worked in the linen business, produce business and then tried to do his own catering business. Then Hurricane Katrina hit, and they were forced to come home.

At first, I was glad to see him more often, until seeing him grew painful. Every time I saw him, he had a beer in his hand. Unlike me, he never discovered his limit, just shot right past it. His wife became his drinking buddy, and his sparring partner, verbal and otherwise. I worried about his four daughters. He adored them, but he also terrified them. Sometimes, in the right light, one or another of them reminded me of our mom. I wanted to protect them. I wanted to help him. But he was my older brother. What could I tell him he didn't already know?

Around the time my business took off, things took a turn for the worse in my brother's house. He and his wife were friends with another couple who developed worse marital trouble than theirs, until one day my brother and sister-in-law invited the wife to stay with them until the trouble blew over. She stayed in an apartment over the garage. Kyle started taking his best buddy's wife on long walks for long talks. Soon the whole house knew, though nobody said, that something more was brewing between those two. Kyle's struggle with his own marriage intensified. In short, the house turned into a mayhem of shouting, crying, throwing, accusing, all fueled by alcohol.

Kyle's eldest daughter, Megan, called my wife and me a couple of times and let small trickles of information leak out, just enough so we got the picture. She had just turned 18 and was desperate to get out of that house, but she had never been on her own before and she had nobody to advise her on how to leave the nest. Her parents were too busy with their own drama.

Annette had recently gone back to work, and she and I had been looking for somebody to help us ferry our kids around to their activities. I don't know who said it first, but we both agreed: "Let's get Megan out of that Looney Tunes environment."

I called Megan. "Why don't you think about coming and living with us? You can go to college, work at Panera, and help us with the kids."

Unlike her dad, Megan did not get emotional in front of people, but now she sounded like she was choking, like someone holding back tears. "Can I really do that, Uncle Keith?"

We made up a room of her own at our house and helped her buy a used car, which she drove to community college to sign up for classes. Within days, I saw a marked change in her. She was like a tightly wrapped bundle after you undo the knot and everything sort of releases, opens up, and softens. I could tell what it was: she felt safe in our home. Safe enough to unfold what had been going on at her house, where it wasn't safe. She suggested, without saying it directly, that she and her father had been in a fight that got physical. She refused to say how far it went, but my protective instinct rose inside me like a grizzly. I was on my feet in an instant, ready to call her father and lay into him, though my wise wife convinced me I needed to calm down first.

Except for my initial retreat from God, and my brief time on the edge of the law, my brother and I had a way of avoiding conversations about anything serious. There was just too much under the surface I didn't want to jostle, and I suspect he didn't want to either, especially all the wounds from our mother's death. But it seemed to me my brother's avoidance of our family's past might be one reason his family was falling apart in the present. I composed myself the best I could—I didn't want to break my relationship with my brother—then I took a deep breath, and picked up a phone.

I stepped inside a closet before I dialed. This needed to be private, between him and me.

"This has to stop, Kyle," I said. "The days of abusing your daughters are over—verbal or otherwise, I don't care. Because if it doesn't stop, I'm kicking your ass."

"You don't know what's been going on here," he said.

I said, "I don't care. It's not okay for your kids to be scared of you. And whatever has been going on over there, I know you have a problem with your temper. I know you, bro."

It sounded like he was crying. I believe he was embarrassed. Maybe I was embarrassed for him. He didn't say it, but reading between the lines of his defensiveness, I sensed he felt he had failed, and knowing that his baby brother was the one taking responsibility to pick up the pieces with his daughter only deepened his sense of failure. Still, I couldn't back off now. Not just for my niece's sake, but for my brother's.

"You need help, Kyle. There's no shame in that. Everybody needs help sometime. I think counseling would be a good idea."

"Keith, I'm not paying a stranger to listen to me talk about my feelings. That's not me."

"If money's the issue, I'm happy to help pay."

"That's not it."

"If not counseling, you've got to do something. Your life's all over the place."

Kyle said he'd rather go to the source of the problem: our dad. If their relationship had been better, he explained, he wouldn't have such a hard time being a good father himself. Our father had moved home to Conroe, too, so Kyle promised to sit down with him and talk things out, to try to build a stronger relationship with him.

After we talked, he did as promised and called Dad to arrange to meet with him for lunch every Wednesday. Together they talked over the past, forgave each other, and built a new bond. Our father offered him advice, and maybe for the first time my brother listened. But if Dad said anything to him about the sanctity of marriage, Kyle didn't act on it.

Within a few months he left his wife, moved to Wisconsin with the other woman, and married her, leaving the rest of his daughters behind with their mother.

***

Megan stuck with us, and seemed to thrive. I did not automatically hand her a job, but got her an interview with the manager of the Panera closest to our house. He gave her an entry-level position as a cashier. At home, I sat her down at our kitchen table for a talk. "You have to stand on your own," I said. "Being my niece is not going to be a positive thing at this job. If anything, it's going to make it harder for you to prove yourself. You'll have to work hard to get ahead."

I didn't interact with her at Panera, not even when I came by to check on operations at the restaurant where she worked. I just shook her hand like I did with every employee. She stopped calling me Uncle Keith anywhere but home. Most of her coworkers had no idea we were related.

Although she was happy to help Annette and me by babysitting the kids or giving them rides when she could, she never did end up being available for much of that. We didn't mind, because she was working full time at Panera and thriving, and she was going to school full time.

Or so we thought.

She got up early every morning and went somewhere, but it wasn't school. At the end of her first semester, we asked about her grades. She confessed she was failing every class. She had been ditching classes, though she didn't say how often. I had only ever attended three days of community college before giving up, so I wasn't about to come down on her with some hypocritical speech about how critical it was to finish school. I knew this was not a moment for anger. Kyle was tough on all his girls, and I didn't want to add to that because I saw how it had crushed her self-confidence, though I knew that wasn't what my brother had intended. The last thing she needed was her uncle to make her feel worse than she did.

I knew she felt bad. She couldn't look me in the eye.

Still, she needed guidance, needed a push in the right direction, and since she was under my roof, I was going to give it to her. This kitchen-table talk was more serious than the last one.

"Look, Megan, I'm just disappointed because I feel you haven't been honest with us. Integrity is important."

"I'm sorry I let you down, Uncle Keith. I just didn't know how to tell you. The thing is, I've never been good at school."

That I understood. "School isn't everything, Megan. You don't have to feel like college is a checklist thing. You'll know what you're supposed to do when you know it."

"All I've ever known is restaurants. That's what I'm good at."

"Okay, why don't you stay with that then? You can always go back to college. Maybe school isn't your thing. Who knows, maybe the restaurant business *is*. If so, then work hard at it. Everyone should find out what they're good at, and work hard at it. Finding something you can be passionate about and throwing yourself into it: everyone should experience that."

Megan took my advice. She stuck with Panera and soared. She took the initiative to learn every position in her store until the manager promoted her, first to shift supervisor, then to assistant manager. On her own time, she joined a church group and made friends.

Once she advanced into management, I sat her down for a final talk at our kitchen table. "Megan, it's time to move out on your own. You're twenty years old. You're an adult. You can't live in our house forever. I know you can make it out there. You've already proven yourself."

So, she moved out and found an apartment. But she stayed at Panera. Every promotion she got, she earned. The area manager wanted to promote her to general manager at the next store that came available. I said no. I wanted to avoid favoritism.

He said, "But she's good, man."

I said, "Let me think about it."

***

Kyle and his new wife were not doing so well. Once again, Kyle found himself married to a drinking buddy and sparring partner. She kept calling her ex-husband, maybe because her son was still living with him, or maybe because she was having second thoughts, maybe both. She started telling people she was going to divorce Kyle.

In March of 2012, he called me for an unrelated reason. He said he had a great idea. "I'd like to write your story, Keith."

"My story?" That wasn't what I expected.

"I've been trying to get back into my writing, but I'm blocked. And I realize, everything that comes up is just too dark. I'm just wading through shit right now and I need something to get me through it. What I need is a bright story to write about, and you've got one."

"One what?"

"A bright story. You've always said you wanted to share your story at some point, about how you almost ended up in prison but then turned your life around. It's a great success story, Keith. But, you know, you never did learn how to read or write. You need someone to write it for you, and that's what I do. Let's do this together."

The idea tempted me, but my brother's tone did not. He sounded desperate, irrational, grasping at straws. "Someday, maybe. But this isn't the right time."

"Why not?"

"It sounds too self-serving, talking all about me. Nobody wants to hear that crap: 'look at me, look what I did, look how important I am.'"

"You're wrong," he said. "That's not what it is at all. It's inspiring. People need to know that if they screw up, there's still hope. It's the perfect story."

"You just want to avoid your own life."

"Well, sure. Wouldn't you if you were me? That doesn't mean it's not a great story."

"No, bro. I'm not ready."

"I need this."

"Well, I don't," I said, or maybe I just thought it. I only know I hung up on him.

Not long after that, he emailed me a list of eighty-six questions about my life. The email began:

In lieu of a face-to-face meeting (due to geography) I wanted to give this a try. Just hit reply and answer the questions in the body of the email. This is just a start...

Some of the questions made me uncomfortable, like: *What motivated you shortly after Mom died?* Others ticked me off, like: *Describe the City of Conroe experience and any other attempts at work during this period. What were you earning and what was your job? How did you screw it up?* Others just left me at a loss: *In the cycle of transformation, compare yourself to Keith Isbell in 1985.*

The next day I sent a polite reply:

Before we move forward and spend any time on this, I need to be sure this is the right thing for me. I want to bounce it off a couple of others first. Thanks for your willingness to take this on, I just don't want to waste your time if it isn't the right time.

I decided it felt too weird, my own brother writing my story, just another of his hair-brained schemes. I knew he was afraid I didn't take him seriously. I guess maybe I didn't. There was always a slight tension between us, and it seemed different than the usual big brother-versus-little brother issue. Even though he was older than me by four years, he once said, "Sometimes I feel like I'm the younger brother. It's like you're the big success, and I'm the one who looks up to you, like I'm the dumb kid who can't get it right." Now that we were grown up, I was the one always holding his feet to the fire, instead of the other way around.

I never wanted to hurt his feelings though, so I avoided getting back to him about the book. He could not take a hint. He kept emailing me about it until I flat-out told him to leave me alone.

He did.

The next time I heard from Kyle, he and his second wife were moving back to Conroe. Maybe they hoped to regroup with family support around them. Maybe they wanted to be closer to their kids from their first marriages. Or maybe Kyle was just restless, like always.

***

One Sunday morning, a couple of months after Kyle emailed me his eighty-six questions about my life, a couple of days after he moved home, my dad called. I looked at the clock. It was just after 9:00 a.m. Something was wrong. Dad was always at church at that hour. He was crying, struggling to put words together.

"Dad, I can't understand you."

Finally, I made two words out: "Kyle," and "dead."

"What happened?"

"There was a car accident. Last night. He was with Jack."

Jack was his wife's ex, his former best friend. "Oh my God. Jack killed him?"

"Jack was driving. They were together."

"I don't understand."

"Neither do I. Can you call your sisters?"

My questions had to wait. I got hold of Leslie, but I couldn't find Julie. It was always hard to find Julie. The phone rang again. This time it was Megan. I couldn't understand her either. I exchanged a look with Annette and said, "Megan, honey, don't you move. We're coming right over."

The moment I stepped out of the car at Megan's apartment she was already running toward me. This girl who had not shed a tear since she arrived in Houston was now wailing her heart out. I opened my arms, and she ran straight into them. We stood in the parking lot, her hanging onto me for dear life, me holding her up.

I had no idea what to say, except to repeat, "Your dad loved you a ton."

"I can't believe… I can't believe…" she replied, but never finished the sentence.

Then we stood there without speaking. It wasn't necessary. I was Uncle Keith, the first person my niece always called for help. That's what she needed me to be. It was a single bright moment in the dark.

***

I spent months dealing with the district attorney, piecing together the events that led to my brother's death. Yes, he died in a car crash, but it was no accident. The D.A. said he was sure about that, as did the cop who was on the scene the night Kyle died. She came to his funeral, the cop. While the mourners ate casserole, cried over another loss in our family, and tried to laugh over old memories, I talked with that officer about the last hours of my brother's life.

Here's what I learned about that night:

My brother had only been back home for a week when his former best buddy, who also happened to be his wife's ex-husband, met them both at a bar in Houston. The three of them drank beer for hours.

There's no telling what they talked about. I picture them laughing and pretending it was like old times one minute, making pointed remarks the next, then whispering or shouting lectures to each other on friendship, family, and decency, then back to chumming around again.

At some point, witnesses heard the wife call it a night. She headed back to the hotel where she and my brother were staying while they looked for a place to live. But Kyle and his old buddy agreed, hey, let's keep the party going. For that, they decided on a change of scene and headed to Conroe, where they had grown up together, where I had watched them lead the way into the adult world. The story gets sketchy as to where they went in the coming hours, but they hit at least a couple of other bars and then McDonald's. By then, it was closing in on midnight. In my mind, Kyle said, "Buddy, I'm beat," and asked his inebriated friend to drive him back to the hotel.

That trip took them down I-45. I've seen the next part on

camera, but the video is sort of dark, so the only reason I know they're the ones in the car is because cops ran the license plate. At first, Kyle's old buddy's car is cruising in the fast lane, and it all looks normal. He's not weaving or speeding. Then the brake lights come on, in the middle of the freeway. The car goes out of frame, then pops into view again, headlights now moving the wrong direction: northbound in the southbound lane, hurtling toward oncoming traffic at high speed, only to plow head-on into the first car in its path.

I cringed every time I watched the two front ends connect and crumple.

The two people in the other car died instantly. So did my brother. He was thrown through the windshield because he wasn't wearing his seatbelt. Cops don't know if he failed to buckle up because he was drunk, or if he saw what his friend was doing and tried to jump out of the car.

The driver—Kyle's ex-best-buddy, his wife's ex-husband—survived.

The D.A. charged him with manslaughter. But he was in the hospital for months, and when he was released doctors diagnosed him with traumatic brain injury. The effects have forever impaired his ability to think straight, like a permanent drunk. Thanks to that diagnosis, the D.A. said they could no longer make a case against him, that plus a lack of witnesses who might testify about his intent. The D.A. and every cop I talked to said some version of, "We know it was intentional, but knowing that and proving it are two different things."

The only other thing I know for sure about my brother's death: He had reached out to me, grasping for a story to restore his hope, desperate for a second chance, and now I could never give that to him.

***

Months later, Kyle's daughter Megan called me to say she was having a hard time going on with her life. After the day we got the news, after I hugged her and told her how much her father loved her, we had not talked about him again. I guess neither of us knew what to say. But one day, she called me, caught me on the road. She said she was missing him and it just hit her that she would never talk to him again. I pulled my car over to listen.

"I know he wasn't perfect," she said, "but most of the time he was a good dad, and he loved me, and I was wondering, Uncle Keith..."

"Yeah?"

"Do you think my dad went to heaven?"

There it was. The question I was dreading. Truth was, my brother's death had me questioning it all again: was God real? If so, how could He let such terrible things happen to good people? Just who was this God? But this time I felt it was okay, to ask questions and to not have answers. So instead of telling her what I knew, I talked about what I believed. "I'm not in heaven, so I'm no expert. But here's what I'll tell you, your dad believed a hundred percent that Jesus walked this earth, that He was real, that He died on a cross for all of us, including your dad. That was Jesus' promise. Based on that promise, I absolutely believe your dad's in heaven."

That belief is not always a comfort. My brother made countless mistakes, yet through it all I believed he was a good man. I always knew if I needed him I could count on him to stand up for me, and stand behind me. He knew more about me than any of my other friends or family did. Our mother's death had left a hole. Now the hole was bigger. Our family would never be the same. I would never be the same. How could I? I no longer had a big brother.

My father had been the head of our family, but my mother's death had broken him, and my brother had never known how to fill the void. Now he was gone, so I tried to pick up the baton and run with it, to throw my arms around everybody and say, "We're still a family, and as long as we're here for each other we're going to be okay." Sometimes it feels impossible to hold us together and keep us from flying apart again. But I do the best I can. I try to live the bright story my brother saw in me, to be his second chance, the leader he never got to be, to carry on.

Chapter Sixteen

THE COACH

Train up a child in the way he should go; even when he is old he will not depart from it. - Proverbs 22:6

Zach was about eight when I started coaching Little League. Today, Little League baseball is big business. Back then it was low pressure. At least, that's how I tried to treat it. For me, being assistant coach meant the chance to be a better dad, to bond with my son, whether playing catch in our backyard or standing on the ball field offering tips and cheering him on. Zach was not a great player at first, so I encouraged him, "Let's work harder. Let's practice till we get it right!" That was just how I was wired: competitive. My wife warned me not to get carried away, and I did my best to keep it fun, all about participation, everyone gets a trophy. I refused to become one of those crazy parents screaming from the sidelines. Still, I thought the life lessons available in sports were important. I taught my son the values of teamwork, practice, and excellence.

We kept at it most of the year; the fall season bled into winter, which bled into the spring season. We got forty-five days off in summer. Then it started again.

After a couple of years, when Zach was ten, another baseball dad came to me and suggested we kick it up a notch and start a team for tournament ball: Select, Elite, Premier. That's how kids start on the track toward high school ball, college stardom, maybe the pro leagues. This father asked me to be head coach and offered to assist. I said yes. We played forty-five games and ten tournaments. It started out fun. But the other dad, the assistant coach, came on strong, kept wrestling control from me. He was a dangling nerve. If the kids were off their game, he'd freak out. If the umpire made a bad call, he'd freak out.

One day, one of our kids slid into third, safe, but the umpire called him out. I was no pushover, and I took a couple of steps toward the ump, ready to argue. But the assistant coach ran across the field going berserk, shouting and flapping his arms. In the middle of his tirade, he lay down in the middle of the field to reenact the slide, his way to prove the ump's call was ridiculous. The ump looked embarrassed, not for himself but for my assistant coach, flailing on the ground. I looked away, thinking, *Oh my God, I can't believe a grown man is acting like this.* I would never confront someone that over-amped, for fear I would only make it worse.

After that season, I sent the assistant coach a carefully crafted email to tell him, in so many words: *If you want this team, it's yours, but I'm moving on to start my own team. This partnership is not working for us, and it's not good for our families.* His kid and mine were good friends, even though he and I weren't. I needed to step away before I trapped my son in the middle of a feud.

The guy emailed back and said he wanted to keep the team. I promised not to recruit kids from the existing team, except my own son, plus anybody the other coach didn't want to keep. He assured me the only kid he wanted, aside from his own, was this one stellar player. That boy's parents later told me that when they sat their son down to explain Coach Keith was leaving but that their

184

son was going to stay with the assistant coach—the boy cried. "I want to be with Coach Keith," he said. So, they called the other coach and gave him their regrets.

With that, I still only had three players from our original team. I filled the rest of my slots with kids from across town, most of them from a part of town known for underperforming schools and high crime. The rest of the original team stayed with the other coach or quit. He hired another head coach, and it came to me through the grapevine that he was spreading word among potential recruits: "Keith's team is terrible. It's full of kids nobody wants. My team's better." A few people said that kind of sour grapes was how they knew *not* to put their kids on his team, although some families did listen to him.

I took Annette out for dinner one night, and afterward we sat at the bar to toast my decision, which was proving so right. She said the kids on my team were lucky to have me.

"I still need more recruits," I said.

"A catchy team name might help," she suggested. "You know, we live in Humble, Texas, and Humble's history is all about oil. How about something to do with oil?"

I listened, admiring, as my wife told me all she had learned about our town's past. I understood then how fully she had thrown herself into building a life with me in Texas, a place she had never planned to end up. I thanked God this smart, beautiful, Chicago-born teacher had taken me back.

"Okay then, what's our team called?" I asked, "The Derricks?"

The bartender leaned in. "Why don't you call it The Oilers?"

"Perfect!" Annette said. "We can do baby-blue uniforms like the old Houston Oilers."

All the 11-year-old boys in town wanted to play for our team.

We did not pick them based on proven skill, only on their desire to play. Yet our team played better than 500 ball, won more than we lost. Meanwhile the team I had left behind fell apart, went 4 and 27.

I prided myself on never cutting a kid, although sometimes I wanted to cut a parent or two for pushing too hard. Even though I gave every kid time on the field, some moms hammered me, each one sure her child was too special to wait his turn: "You're not playing my kid enough!" Sometimes those parents pulled their sons off the team. But every time that happened, more kids lined up to take their place.

A lot of tournament organizations charge hundreds of dollars a month for the privilege of playing on their team. That was not the kind of team I wanted. I believed any kid who wanted to play team sports should have a shot. I made it clear I was just a restaurant guy, no expert at baseball, so I never charged a coaching fee. To keep things affordable, we practiced wherever we could find a place that didn't charge a facility fee. Sometimes I asked the kids to bring five bucks for the batting cages, but if they didn't have the cash I didn't sweat it. If you played on my team, you could eat free at any of my restaurants during the season, and man, could those kids eat! For me, restaurants have always been about community, so I never considered that a hardship but a blessing.

After some initial shifting around, we had the same nine kids on our team every season all the way to high school. Most lived near the only Panera where I won't deliver at night because the neighborhood is too dangerous. But only one of those kids ever went off the rails. The others soared, not just on the field, but in school.

We became a family of thirty: players, moms, dads, brothers, sisters, and my new assistant coach, Carlos, the father of the star player who insisted on sticking with Coach Keith. Carlos and I worked together with such conviction and trust that we were not just a coaching team but a brotherhood. As for the kids, it didn't matter what neighborhood they came from, if their family was broke, if their parents were divorced, if they had a dad in prison. "We're a team, no matter what," I said. We prayed before every game. They knew I loved them, because I told them so all the time.

Whenever I gave a pep talk, I did not just teach those boys how to play ball. I told them what the game could teach us about how to live. "The test of a winner is not about what you do when you're at your best, it's about how you react when you make an error. When life gets hard, how do you respond? How quickly can you shake it off? When you're struggling with hitting, do you get paralyzed with 'I can't' or do you hit the batting cages? Playing to win is about overcoming, it's about having faith."

I told them "Anybody who says, 'it's not about winning and losing' probably loses all the time." Zach understood. I was not putting down people who lose. That happens to everyone now and then. I was only suggesting people who win always come from among those people who never give up. To me, a spirit of fun and a spirit of competition go hand-in-hand. I even compete with my neighbor over who gets the garbage to the curb first. If my neighbor puts the garbage out at 7:03, then I'm out there at 7:02, running for it, rolling those bins as fast as I can, both of us laughing. I taught my son that if he was going to compete, then he should compete at the highest level. If that meant he needed to practice his swing an extra 100 times, or practice pitching an extra hour, then that's what we would do.

Zach was not the biggest, the strongest, or the most natural talent. But he pitched over 100 strike-outs by age 13, because he worked it.

Then came ninth grade. Although we had started as a random bunch, most of our players were ready to move on to Showcase ball and high-ranking high school teams, where the coaches were former pro players. I had taught these kids all I could until they surpassed my skill set.

Our last tournament, I gathered them in the dugout for one final pep talk. "Someday, what I hope for you guys is this: down the road, twenty years from now, if you're going through a hard time, I just hope I've said something that sticks in your head, and that it'll be the exact advice you need from me at that moment." I gave them a long look and saw they all had tears in their eyes, which made my eyes mist over till I could barely see them. "One last thing: God willing, someday you're going to be fathers, and if you're ever given the opportunity to coach your son or daughter, do it. You'll never regret it."

Zachary smiled at me through his tears. I didn't want it to end, not only sharing the field with my son, but also sharing so many life lessons with him. A lot of kids blow off their parents' advice: "That's just my dumb dad." But I was the coach, all the kids looked up to me, together we made a winning team, and through it all my boy listened right along with the others.

Zach's freshman year, he moved on to high school ball with the other kids, but we all missed each other. So, in the summer of 2015, Carlos and I decided to bring the boys together for some showcase tournaments. The parents were thrilled. So was the organization we played for, who knew our team had finished its final season ranked number two in the country on a Triple-A level. Their club had a network of tourney directors who could get us in front of college scouts.

I was pumped.

***

One steaming summer afternoon in 2015, at a San Antonio tournament, I was coaching third base. The day was so sweltering, sweat glued my entire baseball shirt to my chest. As the game wore on, I felt lightheaded, unstable on my feet, and short of breath. I knew I was dehydrated. The moment the boys ran in, I ducked into the dugout, drank water, and waited for the feeling to pass.

That sort of woozy feeling had hit me before, but only now and then. Sometimes it happened when I spoke at business meetings. Nerves, I guessed, though I loved speaking in front of people. I would lean against the podium, my chair, or the conference table until it passed, which always happened within a minute or two.

On one of my rare physicals, a doctor had told me I had high blood pressure, and he'd prescribed meds. But my pressure had never gone all that high, and my symptoms had never been all that bad. The meds seemed like overkill, so I'd slacked off. I was in great shape, always active, lifting weights, eating balanced meals. I never got sick.

I polished off a bottle of water while the boys went up to bat. The inning finished, and this time the feeling did not pass. Come to think of it, this had happened a few times in the past few weeks. But if it were serious, I would have passed out by now, wouldn't I? It was maybe 110 degrees, and coaching third base put me in direct sunlight. One water bottle probably wasn't enough, what with all this sweat.

The next time we were at bat, I clutched the fence while I guzzled another bottle of water.

Carlos gave me a long look. "You okay, man?"

"I think I'm dehydrated. I feel kind of lightheaded."

"You don't want to mess with that in this heat. Why don't you sit the next one out? I'll coach third."

"Yeah, maybe, okay," I said, though I hated to quit anything.

After the game, I dropped Zach and three of his teammates at a local amusement park and went back to my hotel room, alone.

I lay back on the bed and felt something twitch in my neck. I recognized the feeling. This was the symptom I had noticed right before I'd scheduled my last physical, the time the doctor diagnosed me with high blood pressure. I pressed my fingers to my neck, and I could swear I felt a bulge, like something in there was surging.

I walked to the bathroom mirror for a look. My face was red. Sunburn? No, it was more than that. "Well, that's no good," I said to my reflection.

I drove to CVS to ask the pharmacist to recommend some over-the-counter meds. I told him my symptoms.

He shook his head, gave me that blank look some people use when they don't want to alarm you, or to give away that they think you're stupid. "I'm sorry, but it sounds like you're having a problem that might have to do with your heart, and for that you have to go to an E.R."

I said, "Okay, will do," like it was no big deal.

I found the closest hospital on my GPS. Thought, *what a great invention, GPS.* Thought about my brother. He had died so young. Why had God spared me? I took a deep breath. I just had a little hypertension. Doctors wrote prescriptions for that. I'd taken medicine before. I just needed more. Lots of people went to the emergency room. It did not mean I was dying. If the pharmacist had been worried he would have called 911 himself.

I walked up to the E.R. receptionist. "I'm having trouble. I think it's my heart." I was pleased with how calm I sounded.

She shot out of her chair, and within seconds I was on an exam table with a blood-pressure cuff squeezing my arm like a python. Apparently in an E.R., the words *heart* and *trouble* are a ticket to the front of the line. My blood pressure was off the charts, something like 220/130.

A doctor said something I translated as: "How's this guy even alive?" Then she said, "You're not leaving till we get your blood pressure down."

For the next three hours doctors, nurses, and techs swept me from test to test. I prayed. I realized Annette didn't know where I was, so I texted her. Our texts went something like this:

Me: I had to get some medication. My blood pressure's a little high.
Annette: Where are you?
Me: Doctor.
Annette: A doctor's office? On the weekend?
Me: Don't worry. I'm fine.

The test results came back. I had trouble following what the doctor said, but every time she said a medical term or listed a stat, she sounded alarmed. She gave me meds, my pressure dropped, and she let me go, but not before she said, "When you get home you need to see your cardiologist. This kind of high blood pressure can be a symptom of bigger problems. And these results... something's not right."

That part I got.

I made it back to the hotel room before Zach. I didn't say any-thing to him. The next day we flew back to Houston. I told Annette it looked like I needed to start taking my blood pressure meds again. I left out the E.R. doctor's words, "something's not right." Then I got busy catching up at work, and put off calling my doctor.

I had survived this long. A few more days wouldn't hurt.

CHAPTER SEVENTEEN

THE WIDOW-MAKER

Come now, you who say, "Today or tomorrow we will go to such and such a city, spend a year there, buy and sell, and make a profit"; whereas you do not know what will happen tomorrow. For what is your life? It is even a vapor that appears for a little time and then vanishes away. – James 4:13 - 15

I bought a blood-pressure cuff. I ate fewer fats and more vegetables, increased my exercise from five days a week to six, set a goal to get more sleep, and tried to listen to Annette when she said, "You're working too hard. Let some things go." The blood-pressure cuff felt like a good-luck charm, like having it might ward off death. I grew obsessed with checking my pressure. It remained elevated, but nowhere near as high as it was the night I went to the E.R. Whatever I was doing was starting to work. I realized doctors are primed to treat every symptom they can with medicine or surgery. I could see it now: the E.R. doc had gotten me all worked up over a minor problem that called for nothing more than a simple lifestyle change.

But even though my blood pressure lowered, it refused to drop to normal. Annette saw me use the cuff and pestered me for numbers, asked what I would want her to do if the tables were turned.

So, a month after my emergency room scare, I went to our family doctor. I didn't have a cardiologist. My doctor did an EKG. It was far from normal. He referred me to a cardiologist. Then I waited another month to make that appointment.

My blood pressure was down the day I saw the cardiologist, but he still wanted to run more tests. Three to be exact. The first two he ran that same day: a calcium-score test, which I passed easily, and the stress test, which I knew I would pass because it involved testing my heart while I ran on a treadmill and I run all the time. I was right.

"I've been working on diet and exercise," I told the doctor. In my mind, I was already halfway out the door.

"That's great," he said.

"So maybe I don't need to do the echo."

"Not so fast," he said. "These episodes you've been having are still a concern. And the echo is very different from these other tests."

The echocardiogram called for a separate appointment because it required me to go to a hospital, where they had more advanced equipment. By that point, I had been feeling better for a few months. The day of my appointment, I drove toward the hospital, pulled into the correct lane to make my U-turn to get to the parking lot, and then I had a thought: everything's going great, the echo is overkill, and I've got a lot of work to do, so I'll just go to the restaurant. Not only were the holidays approaching, Panera's busiest time of year, but Mark and I were getting ready to open a new restaurant. Traffic on the street was light, almost clear, so I got ready to change lanes. Several cars appeared out of nowhere and boxed me in, forcing me to complete the U-Turn toward the hospital. At that point, I figured, why not, I'm already here. I had the echo done, in-and-out. The results would take a day or two, but I knew they'd be clean like the others.

A couple of days later, I had forgotten all about it, when my cardiologist's head nurse called. "Dr. Batista needs to see you."

"Okay, but I'm super busy. Can you just tell me what's up?"

"Sorry, I don't have that information. You really need to discuss it with the doctor."

"Can I just call him?"

She gave me a number. I reached his voice mail. "Dr. Batista, will you please just call me. I'm sorry, but I don't have time to come in."

To my surprise, he called back within minutes. "Mr. Isbell, there's an issue with your echo. One thing: you have a bicuspid valve—you only have two valves instead of the usual three. It's a little unusual, but a lot of people can live with that—"

"Well, that's a relief. When the nurse called, she worried me for a minute—"

"—but that's not your problem. The problem is: you have a 4.7-centimeter aneurism sitting on your aortic arch."

"Okay..." I only had a vague idea of what he was saying, but I knew the word *aneurism* was bad. It seemed to me I'd heard that word recently. Where had I heard it?

The doctor was still talking. "If it ruptures, you'll be dead before you hit the ground. It's called The Widow-maker."

My cousin, Bart! That was where I'd heard the word. The guy who had talked me through the dark days of my separation from Annette, who had sent me long letters reminding me how much I had missed God, who had helped save my marriage. Bart had died in 2012, just four years earlier, of a ruptured aneurism. I remembered thinking, at his funeral, *he's not much older than me.* I remembered thinking, *his poor wife and children.*

"Unfortunately, it's too small to work on now," a far-off voice was saying. "We can't operate until it's five centimeters."

Come to think of it, didn't some guy in our neighborhood die from an aneurism? What was his name? Didn't he just keel over right in front of his kids?

"We'll schedule your appointment for August, because by then it should be big enough to work on." Wait, what? What was the doctor saying?

"Whoa, hold on, so you're saying I have to run around with a time-bomb in my chest? Wait for it to grow bigger than it already is? Can't we just round it to five and do the surgery?"

"No. Sorry. It doesn't work that way."

I could no longer deny I was scared to death. My dad's mother and father had both died of heart attacks. I felt my family history crowding in on me, crushing me to the point I could hardly breathe. I'd feared death ever since watching my mom waste away right in the house where I grew up, in front of all of us, when I was 15. That was why I had not wanted to make the U-turn. I knew that now. But there was no changing lanes to avoid this. Death was no longer the vague fear of some mysterious entity that stole my family's lives: my mother, my grandfather, my brother, my cousin. It was now a reality, and it was coming for me, just when I had finally gotten my life together.

And there was nothing to do but wait.

By the New Year, I felt exhausted. The lightheaded feeling was back. I knew some of this came from the constant anxiety of expecting it around every corner: the end of me. If it happened, I'd be out cold in seconds, the doctor said, dead in minutes. There would be no time for regret. So instead the regret hit me now, every waking moment. Regret for all the past time I'd wasted away from my family, away from God, away from my path. Regret for all the future time I might lose now that I had found those things.

My mind kept screaming at me, *I could die any minute! Why are we waiting?*

A friend offered to send my chart to his brother, a doctor. He reported back what his brother said: "This guy is still up and walking around?" In retrospect, I could have done without his opinion.

My biggest fear was that my kids would see me die right in front of them. But unless I avoided my kids altogether, I had no control over that.

***

One night, I dropped Sophie off at volleyball practice with her eighth-grade team. I left to grab a bite at Subway, then returned to pick her up. During our drive home, I began to feel confused. I couldn't think straight. The streets looked odd, like I'd never seen them before, although I did this drive all the time. I said nothing to Sophie. Figured, no point alarming her. I was able to drive, and we needed to get home. What else could I do? I figured it was anxiety, the stress of worrying that at any moment my aneurism might burst and the car would crash and my kid would die, or see me die, or both. I feared this was somehow all my fault. I gripped the wheel tighter. I would have prayed except I couldn't remember how. It felt like I was losing my mind.

When Sophie and I got home, I called for Annette. She must have heard the panic in my voice, because she burst into the kitchen at a run.

"I cannot think straight," I said.

"What do you mean?"

"I don't know." I could think well enough to know I couldn't think right, but that was it. I looked down at my left arm. It looked and felt disconnected from my body. *Oh no, this is it*, I thought, *the thing ruptured and I'm dying.* What was the thing called? The last coherent words I said were, "We gotta go."

I thought, *I'll be gone in seconds, no I'm going to fight to live if I can, please don't let me die in front of my kid like Mom.* I groped for a miracle though I didn't know the word for that either. I reached for the kitchen table, wanted to grab all the papers stacked there, papers with all the medical information about my heart, but my hands refused to work. I couldn't pick anything up. I moved my mouth and nothing came out. I looked at Annette and Sophie in panic. I was unable to speak.

Sophie was screaming and crying. A sudden calm fell over Annette, though her body switched into high gear. She grabbed the keys, drove me to an urgent care facility. Probably not where we should have gone for this kind of emergency, but it was closest and my guess is that her thoughts were only slightly clearer than mine.

At urgent care, I slogged through a slow-motion film. I could see and hear things happening, but they seemed to be happening to someone else, and I could not form any opinion on what they meant. Annette must have mentioned my heart, or maybe the receptionist had seen patients with my blank look before, because a nurse hustled me into an exam room, my wife close behind. My weeping daughter stayed in the waiting room, which seemed like a good idea, though I'm not sure I knew exactly who she was anymore, only that it felt important to me to protect her. The thing with my left hand and arm kept happening. I couldn't make them work. As for talking, that ability returned...sort of. Problem was, the words that came out were wrong.

"What's your name?"

"Carl."

"What do you do for a living?"

"Baseball."

My wife—though I probably couldn't have come up with that word either—was no longer calm but crying hysterically.

So I stopped answering questions.

A nurse straddled my legs where I sat on a chair, stood nose to nose with me, and spoke loud and firm. "You have to keep talking!"

I stared at my wife, who I knew was important to me even though I couldn't think of her name, but I still said nothing, so she cried harder.

My thoughts were something like, *No, I'm not talking anymore, because it just upsets everyone more and I can't say anything right.* I lifted my hand and made a slicing motion across my neck to indicate, *I'm done.* I felt proud of that because even though I still wasn't able to do what I wanted to do with my left hand, at least the right one was working.

Someone said, "I think he's having a stroke."

A technician tried to give me a test, but his hand kept shaking, which prevented him from inserting something that was supposed to go into some slot in some machine.

I heard him say to himself, "Oh, that's not how you do it."

I thought, *What a bozo.* Then I said aloud, "Do you know what the hell you're doing?"

He turned to me, startled. "Yeah, I know what I'm doing."

"It sure doesn't seem like it."

He got defensive. "No, I've done this before."

It occurred to me we were having a conversation. "You understand what I'm saying?"

"Yeah…"

I grinned. This was an improvement.

Someone was on the phone. They were having trouble finding a hospital with a stroke unit that had room for me. Finally, the Texas Medical Center said they had room. We didn't know at the time, but that was a great place for people with heart problems. Except I appeared to be having a stroke.

I had to go by ambulance. The paramedics put me on a stretcher and rolled me past Annette. She was still sobbing, but this time I was able to comfort her. "I'm gonna be okay, baby."

She looked stunned. "What'd you say?"

"I'm gonna be okay."

I was confused when she only cried harder. Wasn't I saying it right?

In the ambulance, I did a quick mental inventory of my brain and body: *I can think straight, I can feel my arms and legs, I can talk, and, most important, I'm still alive.* So, it wasn't the aneurism. The doctor had said if the aneurism burst I'd be dead within five minutes, the blood would rush to my head and I'd bleed out.

At Texas Medical Center, doctors rushed me to the seventh floor, to the stroke unit, where I spent the night bouncing from test to test. Annette, Zach, and Sophie sat in the waiting room all night. At maybe 9:00 a.m., Annette joined me to talk with the doctor. Preliminary results indicated the stroke was minor. It appeared I was going to survive without much damage.

As for the 4.7-centimeter time-bomb in my chest, it was still there. Maybe it was bigger by now. I could only hope. God, what a strange thing to hope for.

CHAPTER EIGHTEEN

THE IMPATIENT PATIENT

Then Jacob was left alone; and a Man wrestled with him until the breaking of day. Now when He saw that He did not prevail against him, He touched the socket of his hip; and the socket of Jacob's hip was out of joint as He wrestled with him. And He said, "Let Me go, for the day breaks." But he said, "I will not let You go unless You bless me!" – Genesis 32:22 - 26

My doctors called what had happened to me a TIA, transient ischemic attack, commonly known as a mini-stroke. Unlike an ischemic attack, which is the most common type of stroke, in a TIA the blood clot is only temporary, so the loss of brain function is only temporary. But the doctors explained this was no reason to take the event lightly. One in three people who have a mini-stroke go on to have a major one. Between my TIA, the aneurism expanding my aorta like a balloon, and my two-for-the-price-of-three heart valves, I felt like my cardiovascular system was in the eye of a perfect storm. All seemed calm come morning, but it was a false calm. Anything could blow at any moment.

An orderly wheeled me downstairs for an MRI of my head. I was lying on the table of the magnetic resonance imagining machine, waiting, when the tech walked in.

"Your name's Isbell?"

"Yeah."

He cocked his head at me. "Where'd you grow up?"

"Conroe."

I was about to ask if this was another test of my brain function, when he asked, "Did your dad coach baseball?"

"Yeah, he did." I studied the guy's face. He didn't look familiar. Did I know him? Had the mini-stroke made me forget him?

He smiled. "You and I were best friends in third grade. I'm Eddie."

"Oh yeah…" A vague face from boyhood flickered through my memory. It had been more than thirty years. No wonder I'd forgotten. I grinned, sat up, and shook his hand.

"Your dad was a great coach," he said. "Man, I idolized him."

"Me too," I said, though that was from another life.

"They said you had an aneurism."

"Yeah, I do."

"You might be in luck. The number one heart surgeon in Texas, maybe the whole country, is in this hospital right now: Dr. Estrera."

"Really? Number one, huh? How do I hook up with this guy?"

He shifted his body, like he was either struggling for an answer or regretting he'd brought it up. He shrugged. "Sorry, I've got no idea. He's a teaching professor. He's always tied up with students. I'm just a tech. Maybe you could ask your nurse."

A short time later, back in my room, I blurted to my nurse, "James, I know I'm getting outta here soon, but can I ask you something? What's up with this Dr. Estrera?"

"Oh yeah, he's a big deal, writes books, does conferences, teaches."

"Okay, I want to meet him."

"You and half the people in this hospital. I'm just a nurse. That's not really something I can arrange."

"Do you know who can?"

He suggested I talk to my doctor, who gave a low whistle. "He's the most sought-after cardiothoracic surgeon in the country. It's not like he has a wide-open schedule."

By this point, I was tired of hearing how great this guy was. I had a potentially fatal heart condition, and the best heart surgeon around was in the same hospital as me. I ran a successful company, and I'd gotten there by doing what it took to make things happen. It was time to put those skills to work. I called my restaurant at West U., not far from the Medical Center, and asked for the manager.

"Look," I said, "don't panic over what I'm about to tell you—I'm doing fine—but I'm in the stroke unit at the Med Center, and I need you to bring catering for 100 people. I'm on the seventh floor. Ask for Nurse James. He won't be expecting you."

"The stroke unit? Uh…okay…all right. Nurse James, got it. But, if he's not expecting us, what do we tell him?"

"Nothing. Just drop off the food and take off."

"Whatever you need, we're on it. Will do, Keith."

Forty-five minutes later, James popped his head into my room. "Mr. Isbell, I have six people here from Panera with more food than we have patients or staff. I'm not sure what to do with all this food."

"Really?" I winked. "Well, why don't you see if Dr. Estrera will come in and have a sandwich?"

James gave me a knowing grin. "I'll go invite him personally."

A few minutes later I heard a commotion at the nurse's station, and through my open door caught a glimpse of an entourage of doctors. I heard someone say Dr. Estrera's name, then mine.

Moments later, a young white-coated doctor I had never seen before walked into my room. "I understand we have you to thank for this great spread from Panera."

"Happy to do it, Dr. Estrera."

"I hear you own Panera."

"Just in Houston. I hear you're the best heart surgeon in the country."

"Just in Texas. I also hear you have an aneurism."

"You heard right, Dr. Estrera."

"How big is it?"

"Two months ago it was 4.7."

He stepped up to the foot of my bed, picked up my chart, and studied it. "Not anymore it's not. It's now 5.1 centimeters. Are you here for surgery?"

"No, I'm here for a stroke. I'm not scheduled for surgery on the aneurism till August."

"That's months away. You could be dead by then."

"That's what I keep saying."

"I'll tell you what, what do you say to me doing your surgery?"

"That's right, I hear you do my type of surgery." I could see James outside the door, smirking and shaking his head. "I'd sure be grateful if you could help me out, doc."

"Who's your cardiologist?"

I told him.

"He's a good doctor."

"Yes, he is. But I hear you're the best."

He chuckled. "I've heard that too. And I hear your sandwiches are the best. Let me go grab one while I look over my schedule for you."

Turned out he was heading to China that night to give a

presentation the next day, and then he was going on a three-week vacation. He had only stopped into this hospital for a couple of hours before heading out. If I hadn't had my mini-stroke the night before, if my old friend from third grade had been on duty an hour later, if I had hesitated about having food delivered, I would never have met Dr. Estrera. We scheduled the surgery for his return, three weeks later.

"I'm coming in Sunday," he said. "Your surgery appointment will be Monday morning."

I thought about it. "Not to look a gift horse in the mouth, but don't you have to fly from tomorrow back to yesterday just to get here from China?"

"It's a long flight across the International Dateline, yes."

"If you're going to be on a plane all night, I'd just as soon you have a day off before you do my surgery. Let's do it Tuesday, so you're well rested when you slice me open."

He shook my hand. "Sounds like a good idea, Mr. Isbell."

"Oh, I'm full of those, doc."

"I don't doubt it."

***

One day in mid-April, my dad and my wife stood on either side of my hospital bed, doing their best to act like we weren't saying goodbye, even though we all knew this surgery guaranteed nothing and we might never see each other again this side of heaven. But if I was about to die, and these were the last two people I was going to see, I couldn't ask for better. At least I was not going to collapse and die in front of my kids, and for that I was grateful. If I got to see my mom and brother again on the other side, even better.

Before I knew it, I was shivering under bright lights with a slew of doctors, nurses, and technicians surrounding me. Who knew it took so many people to care for one heart? I closed my eyes and started to thank God for putting Dr. Estrera and me in the same hospital at the same time. Before I could also thank God for the chance to survive, the anesthesiologist asked me to count back from ten, and somewhere between nine and eight I was gone.

***

Dr. Estrera had told me the surgery would take about four hours, but my artery needed more repair than expected. At one point, something punctured or tore or blew and I wouldn't stop bleeding, so I needed a transfusion. *Complications* was the word doctors said to Annette, but to her it must have sounded like *disaster*. The surgery took eight hours, twice as long as anticipated. I can't imagine how each additional hour must have felt to my wife. For me, though, it was as if no time passed at all.

It had been morning when I went into surgery, but when I woke the lights were dim overhead, and the night was black outside the window. I heard a constant hum of machinery and shuffle of people, but all of it sounded hushed. I was in the ICU. It was only when I took all this in that I realized part of me had not been at all sure I would wake up again.

Annette floated into view, kissed my forehead, and took my hand. I couldn't talk because my throat was raw from anesthesia, but I held up a shaky hand and wrote in the air with an imaginary pen.

"You want to write something?" she asked.

I must have nodded. She walked away and came back with a

lined yellow legal pad and a pen. I wrote in an almost illegible scrawl: *I lived.*

I still don't remember doing or saying any of that, but Annette saved the paper.

I do remember I felt thirstier than I ever had in my life. The ICU nurses were angels, but at first it was hard not to hate them because they wouldn't give me water, just ice chips. I begged Annette to break the rules and give me a sip of water.

"The nurses say you can't drink water yet. You'll throw up."

"Baby, please, I just gotta get some water." My voice came out in a pitiful croak.

Annette snuck a cup and straw to me when the nurses weren't looking. I drank two sips and instantly threw up so violently I thought my feet would come out my mouth. My diaphragm felt like it was on fire.

"That's why you're not allowed to drink water," Annette said.

I nodded, hating her too at that moment, even though I knew it wasn't fair.

All the gratitude I had felt going into surgery vanished. I was, quite possibly, the worst patient my nurses ever saw.

To recover from heart surgery, it's critical for patients to get out of bed and sit up for so much time each day. I refused. In my defense, part of the problem was that I couldn't handle morphine, or any of the other pain meds they tried on me, without puking. I was only taking Tylenol, which was kind of a joke for dealing with the pain I felt after having my chest cracked open and surgeons running their hands around inside me.

"I can't sit up," I complained. "I'm in too much pain."

"I understand," the nurse said. "But if you don't start sitting up you could get an infection, and then believe me, you'll be in much worse pain. You have to sit up, Keith."

"Honey, it's for your own good," Annette said. "Please, do what the nurse says."

"No, I'm just going to lay here."

"There's some kind of confusion, here, Keith," the nurse said. "You're not in charge."

"I'm in charge of me. So just move along to the next room."

Instead of leaving, she took my pulse. It was too high.

"I'll make you a deal," she said. "If you'll sit up for thirty minutes, just call me and I'll come right back down here and put you back in bed."

"Okay," I said, against my better judgment.

I sat in a chair next to the bed, watching the clock the entire time, and hit the call button exactly thirty minutes later. The nurse didn't come at a run, so I kept pressing the button.

I shouted at Annette, "That nurse lied to me!"

Annette tried to calm me down, but I wouldn't listen. All I knew was she was not helping and did not appear to be on my side, which only made me madder.

An assistant came in, and I shouted at him, "Can you go find my nurse?"

"Don't worry, she'll be back in a few minutes. Just be patient."

"So you're in on it too."

"It's not a conspiracy, Keith," Annette said. "It's only been a couple of minutes."

I kept looking at the clock. At thirty-five minutes, I said, "She's still not here. I'm putting myself back in bed. Annette, help me."

"No. The nurse and the doctor both told you that you can't stand on your own yet."

I tried to stand, fell over sideways, and could not get up. "Annette, help me!"

"Oh, for Pete's sake." She walked out.

The nurse returned, but my wife didn't. I was half on and half off the bed, my face smashed into the pillow. "Mr. Isbell, just what do you think you're doing?"

"You lied to me."

"I've been busy, Mr. Isbell. You're not my only patient."

She helped me into bed, gently adjusting my body while verbally punching me out.

I continued to resist the doctors' and nurses' orders whenever those orders didn't suit me. I was in so much pain it felt like I'd been run over by a truck, and I took it out on everyone who came near. I had survived the surgery, but I was not sure I would survive the ICU.

Some people don't. Sometimes patients have successful surgeries and still die afterward. I knew that.

I didn't feel grateful anymore. Not. At. All.

CHAPTER NINETEEN

THE HEART PILLOW

This is the day the Lord has made; We will rejoice and be glad in it. – Psalm 118:24

The surgeon had warned me it was normal after heart surgery to spend three days in the intensive care unit. I was still there on day four. My heart fibrillated at one point, beating at over 200 beats per minute, when a normal sinus rhythm is 60 to 100. The ICU doctors and nurses did not even try to pretend they weren't freaked out. Machines beeped, people scurried, talking fast, almost shouting. They gave me medication that calmed my heart rate down. That was just one hurdle.

My digestive system refused to wake up from the anesthesia, so after I started eating, I could not digest any of my food or eliminate the resulting waste. That meant whatever I ate sat parked in my stomach, rotting for all intents and purposes. That decomposing food threatened to become toxic. They had to stick a tube down my throat for twelve hours to pump my stomach so all those toxins wouldn't poison me.

At another point, I stood up, accidentally stepped on the tubes that were draining my post-surgical wounds, and ripped them from my chest. So much blood spurted everywhere it looked as if I'd been shot.

Even though the nurse won her initial battle to get me to sit up, I continued resisting her. All I wanted to do was lie down. The day she said it was safe for me to eat, I felt too disheartened to try. For a guy used to taking charge and getting things done, it was a quick slide from feeling physically broken to emotionally broken.

At my sickest, I mentally planned my own funeral. I thought most about my eulogy. I wondered who would talk about me, what I hoped they would say. What did I think my life meant? I thought about all I had accomplished, and I was pretty proud. Then I got to thinking about the people I loved, and how I had only recently prioritized spending time with them: my wife and kids, father and siblings, even my friends. It all felt too little too late. By day five in the ICU, I feared I would die before I had a chance to do more. *I need more time*, I thought. I decided, if I survived this, I would commit to living a life worthy of the eulogy I wanted.

"What do I want my eulogy to be about?" I asked myself. Not about financial success, which was all well and good, but look where I was. I had seen money as necessary for survival, as security for my family, as a symbol I was a leader among men. Yet money had not prevented me from ending up face-to-face with death, threatening my wife and kids with the loss of a husband and father, leading me to a place where nobody wanted to follow. Money had provided me opportunities to do great things, but that wasn't what made my life matter. What mattered most to me were my family, friends, community, and the opportunity to be a positive force in the lives of everyone who crossed my path.

With that, I knew I wanted to get home to start my recovery: physical, emotional, and spiritual. Stuck in the hospital, I was on the hospital staff's agenda, and having them tell me what to do all day long was wearing on my spirit. My first step was to get out of the ICU. With that decision, my body rallied. Still, I didn't break out overnight.

My determination to throw myself into a life of serving others did not stop me from taking my frustrations out on those who were serving me. Where before I had fought the doctors and nurses, especially the nurses, with my stubborn refusal to get out of bed, now I fought them with my stubborn refusal to stay in it. I wanted to get the hell out of bed and out of the hospital, for good. Every day Dr. Estrera came in to check my progress, and every day he held up one finger. "One more day."

Every day I replied, "So you keep saying. You're a liar." I was only half kidding.

After eight days, he gave the okay for me to go home. A nurse told me there were procedures they had to follow to release me, which could take up to eight hours. "Oh no it won't," I told Annette. I called a friend who knew a couple of hospital administrators. "Please get me out of this hospital!"

In less than an hour, an orderly with a wheelchair appeared at my door and wheeled me out of the hospital to our waiting car.

I felt like I had escaped a trap as Annette drove me away. Now I could do what I wanted.

***

Everything I wanted to do was so much harder than I imagined. It felt like I was the victim of a mean prank, like someone had stolen my body and replaced it with that of a 100-year-old man, who had been flattened by a steamroller, more than once.

After my surgery, nurses gave me a heart-shaped pillow to clutch to my chest most of the time. My sternum had been sawed open, and the pericardial membrane that used to encase my heart had been torn, so everything in my chest felt too close to the surface. The mere act of breathing felt like it could split open my sternum. Pressing the heart pillow to my chest created the sensation of holding everything in place. Whenever I coughed or stood or walked, I clutched that pillow to me. It made me feel more comfortable and less vulnerable. All the signatures on the pillow reminded me of why I had survived, what I had to live for:

Get better soon, Zach
Best Dad ever, Sophie
You did it! Probably the hardest eight days of our marriage and your life, but you're tough as nails. Keep looking up. What a ride! Love Annette
Little brother I love your heart with all of mine, love Leslie

Still, part of me felt reduced to nothing but that pillow. Back in my own home, away from the nurse tyrants—who were really angels though it was tough to see that then—I was now in theoretical charge of myself. But as I made the long slow walk to my own bed, my physical limitations overwhelmed me. My mind felt free, but my body was slow to follow. This reality hit so hard it knocked the wind out of me. I clutched my pillow tighter.

My first morning at home the heart pillow was lying on the chair next to our bed, and it was all I could do to get out of that bed, walk two steps to that chair, sit down, and clutch the pillow while I gasped for breath. I thought, that's it, I don't have any more in me. Then I scolded myself, *No, stop that.* I've gotta start thinking about what I *can* do instead of what I *can't* do. I spoke the next part out loud: "Get up."

214

I refused to dive back into the despair of my long, dark stay in the ICU. Instead, I leaned into the one strength I knew I still had: I could set goals. To take my focus off all the things I couldn't do, I would make a list of all the things I *could* do. I rose slowly, shuffled to my office, sat at my desk, and did my morning devotional to God. This was a habit I had acquired shortly before discovering my aneurism. It seemed a good place to start. I usually studied a Bible passage, but I felt too wound up to read, so all I could manage for the moment was to breathe a small prayer of gratitude. Then I grabbed a pen and paper, and made my list of can-do items:

take a walk
make breakfast
take a shower

It was a short list.

That did not mean it was easy. I shuffled to the closet, put on my shoes, picked up my heart pillow, and headed out my front door for the first of three 15-minute walks for the day. I walked so slowly I not only felt a hundred years old but must have looked it too. I didn't give up, though, until I finished the full fifteen minutes.

For lunch, I could barely open a bag of bread to make a sandwich. Who knew that task used so many muscles? But I did it.

On day one, Annette had to help me take a shower because I could not lift my hands above my shoulders. On day two, I was determined to shower on my own. I figured out that if I got down on my knees in the shower, the water would fall straight down over my head and shoulders, so I wouldn't have to reach up. Annette shook her head, laughing. But I did it.

Every day my to-do list added something that sounded simple

but always ended up a bigger challenge than I imagined. Like: "Do the laundry." That didn't look like much, but I was surprised how hard it was to pick something up and put it somewhere else without the ability to bend at the waist or turn my neck. Then, once the clothes were wet? It felt more like weight-lifting than doing laundry. I gave up loading them into the dryer all at once, and instead picked up one item of clothing at a time. It took twenty-plus minutes to load the dryer. But I did that too.

Five days after I got home I added, "Go to work," to my list of things I could do. I couldn't manage that one alone. Annette drove me the one hour to Sugarland to visit one of my restaurants that was undergoing remodeling. The managers' jaws unhinged when they saw me. "What are you doing?!"

I explained that I knew they were doing a great job on their own and I promised not to get in the way. "It's just important to me to get back into some kind of routine as soon as possible. I'm losing my mind at home, and let me tell you, I do not think that's good for my recovery."

They didn't need me. I needed them. I needed to achieve this goal, to feel myself making progress, and to give myself positive fuel to reach my next goal. I only stayed thirty minutes.

"Drive my car" made it onto my list about two weeks post-surgery. I was not supposed to do that one, but I did anyway. I drove to the bank. I'll admit it was probably unsafe. Not only was I still unable to turn my head, but I also remained lightheaded for months. Still, even if that drive was ill advised, the strategy of goal-setting was saving my life. I don't think I could have survived those months of limitation and frustration without it. It never escaped my thoughts that I had come close to dying. I didn't want to lose one moment of living.

Every day, somewhere on my can-do lists, I included walking. At first, I had a goal to walk a little farther each day. But one day, about five weeks post-surgery, I sat down to put my shoes on and this heavy, defeated internal voice told me, "You can't do it."

I looked back at my bed with longing, then down at my shoes. In that moment, I made a choice to outwork the defeated voice in my head. I was only supposed to walk fifteen minutes at a time, which meant a block at most. Instead, I shoved my feet into my shoes, grabbed my pillow, flung open my front door—as much as a guy with 10 inch incision in his chest can fling anything—and set out to walk at least three miles through my neighborhood. That was about two dozen times my usual distance per session, six times my usual distance per day.

I did not break any speed records. Anyone who saw me might have wondered if I was going to die right in front of them. I can't remember whether anyone asked if I needed help, but I doubt it. I'm sure my look warned them not to say a word. I sat down a lot, on my neighbors' benches, rocks, and curbs, dizzy and short of breath. About the third time I sat, I decided I could not get up again. It was too hard. I was never going to come back from this.

That's when I decided to talk to God, right there in front of my neighbors' houses. "That's it. No more feeling sorry for myself. What do you say, Lord? Let's think about some things I'm grateful for!" At a loss for where to start, I looked down at my shoes: "Thank you, God, for these shoes." I looked up at the sky: "Thank you, God, for this sunny day." I rose to my feet: "Thank you, God, for the ability to stand." With that, I started walking again, intentionally and constantly staying in that spirit of gratitude.

I had never before spent that much time thanking God. I thanked Him for my pillow, my house, my dogs, my surgeon, my nurses, my wife, my kids, my life. I thanked Him for random things I saw or whatever popped into my head: the sidewalk, hot dogs, hot dog vendors, baseball, grass, flowers, bees, honey. Somewhere along that walk, my internal voice of discouragement disappeared. Those two voices, *gratitude* and *discouragement,* could not exist at the same time in my head. In my new spirit of gratitude, I was able to walk for three hours.

Which was a problem because I'd forgotten my cell phone at home.

Annette was ready to kill me when I walked through the front door. "Where've you been?!"

"Sorry, I forgot my phone."

"You forgot? What the hell were you doing all this time?"

"Walking."

"Walking? For three hours?!"

"Yeah. You see, I had this goal…"

"I didn't know if you were dead or what!" She had tears in her eyes.

"You're right. I'm sorry I worried you. I messed up. It won't happen again, I promise. It's just, I finally realized something. I started walking with gratitude, and it got easier."

She wiped her eyes, and I saw the first hint of a smile. "What are you going on about?"

I explained my epiphany. Annette gave me a big hug, admitted it was wonderful, and told me she was going on all my walks with me from then on. "So at least somebody will be with you if you pass out." I laughed and didn't argue. At that moment, I felt most grateful of all for my beautiful, understanding wife, who knew me so well that she knew I would never stop pushing myself, knew if she wanted to keep track of me she might have to hurry to keep up.

Together, she and I walked three times a day, forty minutes at a time. Then we switched to twice a day, but longer.

***

My goal for eight weeks after heart surgery was to drive my family from Houston to Orlando to visit Disney World. There was a reasonable explanation for this. We had made those plans before the aneurism and stroke. Shortly before I went into surgery, Annette said she was going to cancel Disney World.

I said, "No. Do not cancel that trip. It'll give me something to look forward to."

She tried to reason with me. "Keith, it's not like I'm saying you're not going to make it through surgery. It's just, there's no way you'll recover in time to enjoy an amusement park. You won't be able to do any of the rides."

"No, no, no, let's not talk about what I won't be able to do. This'll help me think positive going into surgery. I need to think past this. Don't even think about canceling. We're going to Disney World!"

The time came for our Orlando trip, and Annette tried to reason with me again. The doctors said I was not ready. I gave her what-for about tattling on me to the doctors, said I knew my body and what it could handle better than they did. She threw her hands in the air and gave in. I didn't give her much choice. At week eight, off we drove.

The only big change in our plans was that we added a stop in New Orleans. We'd done this trip a few times before and normally I drove straight through.

At the park, the first thing I did was turn to my daughter and say, "Let's go to the water park and hit the water slide!"

"Keith," Annette's voice got real quiet, "you shouldn't be doing this."

"I'll be fine, honey. Come on!" I posed my arms like I was challenging my daughter to a race, though I couldn't actually run.

Sophie laughed and the two of us walked on ahead.

I took off my shirt at the slide, and people stared at me like I was a monster. I did look like something Dr. Frankenstein put together. My long cross-hatched chest scar still had blood spots.

I'd be lying if I said that, on the way down the slide, my laughter and shouts weren't just as much from fear as excitement. I hit the water hard, sank straight down, and smacked my rear end on the bottom of the pool. That slam reverberated through my whole body. Terror shot through me for a split second as I wondered, holy crap, did I just do internal damage?!

An instant later I bobbed to the surface and said, "Whoo! That was fun!" Because I did not want to freak my family out.

Annette gave me a look that said I wasn't fooling her, and I gave her a look that said, all right, all right.

I didn't do the water slide again. I still did some rides that jerked me around a bit, including a few that specifically had safety signs to warn people with heart conditions not to board. But what my wife saw as foolhardiness, I saw as a way to remind myself this thing was not bigger than me, or at least not bigger than God. I'll admit, the words "I have a cow's heart-valve inside me" did cross my mind several times as the rides rounded sharp turns and flew down steep drops, but speeding over those rails also helped me fly past my fear of dying.

The thing that threw me for the biggest loop at Disney World had nothing to do with my new heart valve, my bloody wounds, or the wild rides, but instead came from a quiet but stunning conversation I had with my son.

Zach pulled me aside as we walked between park attractions and asked, "How would you feel if I said I don't want to play baseball anymore?"

"Aw, man." As that phrase left my mouth I realized I wasn't surprised. I had been expecting this. I'd always sensed I was more into it than Zach was. Nonetheless, I couldn't help saying, "But Zach, you're really talented."

He said, "Thanks, Dad. I appreciate that. The thing is, I want to be a doctor. And if I'm going to be a doctor, it's going to take a lot more focus on school. Baseball takes up a lot of time, at least at this level."

"When I was your age, I wanted to be a cop. Stop and think about it." I meant what I said about his talent at baseball. I thought it might mean a college scholarship. But a doctor? I knew my son was smart, and a good kid, but this would call for an obsessive amount of work to make it into the top percentile required to get into pre-med and then med school. Was that who he was?

"I mean it," Zach was saying. "This is what I want to do."

"Okay. Who knows? Maybe this is your purpose. If you're passionate about it, then work really, really hard at it. Because everybody should feel what that feels like, to become great at something. I sure can't help you with the academics, but I wish you the best."

I didn't ask him why he wanted to do it. We both knew why. He later told me he wanted to specialize in cardiothoracic surgery, but that didn't surprise me much more than his decision to quit baseball. He had enjoyed baseball because it was something he could do with his dad, and he wanted to be a heart surgeon because a heart surgeon had saved his dad's life.

***

At twelve weeks post-surgery, I took a bigger risk than roller coasters and bench-pressed 100 pounds, five times. Doctors were not a fan of that one. I wasn't stupid about it. I had someone spot me, and I didn't push it, just did a few and stopped. Afterward, I felt great. Not merely like, "Phew, I survived," but more like, "See, I'm going to thrive, and life is going to keep getting better."

Then, at fourteen weeks, I took on my toughest goal of all. This one I had begun planning not long after the surgery, as a celebration of my second chance at life. I took my family on a four-mile round-trip hike to the summit of Enchanted Rock outside of San Antonio. My doctor advised against it, but he knew better than to argue, just asked me to please take a portable heart monitor with me, to make sure my beats per minute never went over 100.

We drove up the night before and spent the night at a hotel so we could get an early start. That was important because it was July. We arrived at the trailhead at 7:30 a.m., and already it was hotter than hell. On top of that, the scenery was not motivating. Enchanted Rock is the kind of bald mountain that looks like nothing more than a giant rock in the middle of the desert. Zach and Sophie were 13 and 15, and, like most teenagers, not skilled at faking enthusiasm. But God love 'em, they maintained a gung-ho attitude most of the way up, and I knew it was all for me. How could I fail to be grateful, even as the steep slopes had me sucking wind like an asthmatic?

Near the summit, I felt more worried about Annette than myself. She's a fit woman, but this was a slog unlike anything any of us had done, even back when I thought I was going to live forever. She teased, "Maybe I should be wearing the heart monitor."

My heart rate never went over 100 BPM's.

The last 100 feet to the summit, a little voice in my head said,

"You've won." This was more than a rock, more than a mountain. Fourteen weeks earlier I had been lying unconscious and split open on a table, as alone and vulnerable as I could imagine a body being. Now I was rising to a summit I'd never attempted before, to look out over God's creation—with my family. This and all my other goals had helped motivate me through unbearable days and nights when I feared I would never be myself again. Now I knew I was more than that, on my way to becoming a better version of myself than I had ever been.

The climb itself was not beautiful, but the views at the top were. We had a 360-degree panorama of the park's trees and creeks spread below us. A cool breeze lifted some of the day's heat. My heart was beating steady and strong, like it did not belong to a patient but to a happy man. I had won this moment because I'd chosen not to focus on what I couldn't do, but on what I could.

"Okay, Dad, we did it! Can we go home now?" Sophie joked.

We laughed with her. Then we all spent some forty minutes up there, celebrating together. Annette and I hugged, the kids high-fived, and we all took photos and videos.

The way down was harder. The heat climbed to 90 degrees, which had me sweating more water than I could possibly take in. We kept losing the trail. But I knew we would make it. I'd never lose faith in that again, because I had witnessed what determination can do.

I asked God to please never let me forget this feeling of gratitude. A week after my surgery, a buddy from high school had a much simpler heart surgery and died on the table. I later had another buddy whose father survived heart surgery, only to have his wife leave him the next day. He never shook the depression that followed. He died a year later.

That sort of thing happens a lot, even to patients whose spouses don't leave. Some people go into the ICU for months and never get out. I discovered a secret to recovery: the body cannot lead the mind; the mind must lead the body. I used my mind to set the goals that got me through this. Even then, I almost didn't make it, not when I tried to power through on my own. I had to put my mind in God's hands to achieve my goals. I had to ask God to show me the way to gratitude.

I never assumed just because I set goals and prayed that my survival was guaranteed. I never forgot I could die any time. But I chose to set goals to prove I could also live at any time.

My doctors often said, "Stop! You don't need to do all that stuff!"

My response was, "I'm not doing it for you. I'm doing it because I need to be on the other side of my fear."

I learned doubt can beat the hell out of me if I let it. My job as I saw it was to do what it took not to let doubt take over. And the opposite of doubt—is faith.

Mostly what changed for me was my perspective, how I saw my life, my family's life, the lives of strangers. I began to wish everybody could see the world the way I did, though maybe without the near-death experience.

Before my aneurism, I had come back to a life of faith. But only after my aneurism did I begin to understand what it might mean to put God front and center. After that day atop the mountain, I felt His incredible grace. My heart had been opened and fixed in more ways than one.

I felt compelled to tell everyone my story so it could impact the world, came to believe this was what I was meant to do. I came to see that the three most important things in my life were family, faith, and legacy. I wanted to leave something in the world that would outlast me. I began to share my testimony, talking to people about my journey from near death to total gratitude. I spoke at my church, gave leadership talks to youth groups, wrote an article for the American Heart Association.

Gratitude is not a new idea, but sometimes it takes jumping a painful hurdle to wake us to our blessings. One day I needed God's help to walk, and His answer was to give me gratitude. After that, whenever I heard an inner voice of doubt, my mind automatically switched to a spirit of thanksgiving. I would pray, "I'm so thankful for a God that loves me, for my family, my friends, my business..." Whenever I did that, doubt fled in a heartbeat.

A 4.7-centimeter bubble in my aorta became the most brutal challenge of my life so far. When a doctor first told me my aorta could explode and kill me at any moment, I felt reduced to near nothing. I felt that way again when I had the stroke and heart surgery. And yet again after surgery, when my strength was reduced to nothing but clutching a heart-shaped pillow. Yet I wouldn't trade any of those moments for the world, because within them I found my life's formula for true perspective: when in doubt, give thanks. That kind of perspective always comes in handy sooner or later.

CHAPTER TWENTY

THE ENEMY

The thief comes only to kill and destroy; I have come that they may have life and have it to the full. – John 10:10

For Christmas 2016, my family and I spent the holidays at the Gaylord Palms Resort, to enjoy their water park, Disney World, and other warm-weather fun. Life was back to normal, with the added bonus that I was still high on daily gratitude, even as I did mundane things like stand in our hotel bathroom shaving for another day of fun with my family. Then I ran the razor over my neck and noticed a small bump. I figured it was a swollen gland, so I went to Walgreens for some over-the-counter medicine for sore throat, just in case. Within a few days, the bump seemed bigger, and now my throat was sore.

"I think it's strep," I told Annette. "Maybe I should see a doc for some antibiotics."

She felt the bump. "Nah, I don't think it's strep throat. You should go see an ear-nose-throat specialist, just to be on the safe side."

I've learned to listen to my wife when she sounds that certain, so I went to the specialist. He didn't bother with the best-case/ worst-case scenarios, just said flat-out, "This looks like cancer." He biopsied some of my throat tissue right then and there, and said it would take a few days to get the results. But I knew. I was no longer the cocky guy who insisted I was fine when it was clear I wasn't. More than that, I'd been waiting for this particular enemy to arrive ever since it killed my mother.

The doctor called me in to discuss my results, and I brought Annette along because I knew the doctor would not call me in without offering any clues on the phone unless the results were bad. He wouldn't look at me when we walked into his office. If I wasn't sure before, I was now.

"Keith, I'm sorry to tell you this is cancer, squamous cell carcinoma. We don't know yet how big it is, or how much it's spread, but it's in your throat and in your lymph nodes. We just know it's far enough along to be aggressive."

I found out later the initial tumor had already pushed deep into my throat. It was 3.7 centimeters, which didn't sound all that big at first, but the doc explained that in that part of the body 3.7 centimeters was considered invasive. It was already sending tentacles in multiple directions: it was reaching into the spot where my tonsils were removed when I was a kid, wrapping around my left ear, and approaching my spine. My cancer was Stage 4. I'd heard that number before. That was the stage most people don't recover from, the stage that kills, the stage that killed my mother. I was stunned, scared, and pissed off.

The doctor launched into explaining the aggressive treatment I needed to undergo to have any chance against this invader: heavy doses of chemotherapy to poison it, accompanied by heavy doses of radiation to burn it, both treatments simultaneous to wage all-out war on this fast-moving tumor. The trick was to kill the cancer without killing me—a familiar story that only felt strange because now it was *my* story. Some of the side effects I'd heard on medical TV dramas, others were a surprise; all of it gave me the feeling this might be a good time to leave my body: "You can expect to lose a lot of weight, lose your hair. For a while you'll lose your taste buds and your ability to swallow, so you'll need a feeding tube. The chemo will cause extreme nausea, and the radiation will cause painful burns. I'm not going to lie to you: the kind of chemo we're talking, the side effects are bad. It takes seven weeks, and a lot of people modify out of the treatment, because not everyone can handle it."

Annette was crying. I didn't blame her. We had already been through so much. She'd faced the prospect of losing me once, twice if we counted the time I left her. She must have found it impossible to believe we'd make it through a third threat. Even for me, those first moments felt like too much to bear. Cancer, to me, was another face of Satan. This was the monster that had tried to destroy my faith. But somewhere within those thoughts, my faith returned, the faith my mother had taught me as a boy. I was still angry, but that was good: I would let God use my anger to defeat Satan, to defeat my fear, to defeat cancer. The fact I had already been through so much and come out the other side was not reason to doubt but to believe.

I felt such certainty about that, I turned to Annette, took her hand, and said, "I want to tell you something. We're going to have to go through something very difficult. I'm going to have some days that for you will be difficult to watch, and for the kids to watch. But what I want you to know is that, come June, I'm going to be cancer free. So, on my worst day, no matter how bad it is, keep your eyes and the kids' eyes on June."

She gave me an exasperated look I knew well, a look that said: Oh, here Keith goes again with his rah, rah, we-can-do-it baloney!

In return, I shot her a knowing look that said, hey, I gotta be me!

I'd barely finished recovering from open-heart surgery, a bad time to put my body through more hell, but cancer didn't give a damn about my schedule. I decided to treat cancer with the same disrespect it was showing me. A couple of days after I found out I had cancer, I went on a 12-mile run. I wanted the cancer to know who it was up against, that my last fight had not left me too battle fatigued to fight again, that if anything it had only trained me in the power God gave me to overcome.

My attitude was: I know why you're here. I watched you kill my mom, my friends, and countless others. If you want me, you have to come get me. I'm ready to fight you.

After that run, everything for the next few weeks was a blur.

***

Though I had no problem with my first doctor, I switched to an ear-nose-throat specialist (or ENT) who was recommended by my heart surgeon for my particular situation. My new ENT, my oncologist, and my radiologist worked as a team to coordinate my treatment.

Dr. Micky Coe, my radiologist, was a spitfire of a woman who didn't mince words. "We've gotta get you started right away."

"Uh, is it bad?"

Dr. Coe looked me in the eye, which I appreciated. "The tumor is sitting on your spine, and if it gets in there it's going everywhere. But we're not going to let that happen."

I saw Dr. Coe almost every day, because every day was radiation day. I often saw my oncologist in between, but within three weeks

I was so sick and disoriented that half the time I couldn't focus on what he said, and it's pointless trying to recall it now.

What I recall most about those days was this: I went to one building to do my radiation, but for chemo I had to walk across the street, trudge past three large buildings to the building where I got chemo, take a slow elevator ride to the fifth floor, and drag my exhausted butt through a door with a tag on it that read, "Multipurpose Room." That name offered a clue to just how careless and half-assed that room felt: as if it really was for any old purpose at all, as if the hospital considered the eight cancer patients who sat there every day nothing but an afterthought. We curled up in pain on uncomfortable 30-year-old chairs, surrounded by blank walls that hadn't been painted in years, crowded together like factory-farmed chickens without an ounce of privacy or dignity.

The Multipurpose Room was actually the infusion room, otherwise known as the chemo room, which I sometimes thought of as the poison room. The place looked intimidating, the kind of place where hope dies, not just because we knew its purpose but because there was not one comfortable, comforting, or welcoming object in sight. It was a hard place to be. My chemo port was installed on my forehead, a couple of other men had theirs on their groins, a couple of women had them on their breasts. Needles stuck out all over. Men waddled off with a nurse to the bathroom to drop their pants and get their port. One guy shuffled back from the bathroom, tripped over his tubes, and fell sprawling onto the floor. More than one woman's breast was exposed to all of us while a nurse installed her port. Everyone threw up in front of everyone else. Sometimes we chatted and cheered each other, but more often we averted our eyes to give much-needed space to each other and our loved ones.

I'm no doctor or psychologist, but I have a strong protective instinct for people, and I didn't need to be an expert to understand that walking to hell and back to get to this chemo set-up that felt like a storage closet, was no good for anyone's mental or physical health. More than that: the whole experience was humiliating and inhumane. It didn't take long before I thought of my fellow chemo patients like a kind of family. Which made it hurt more to see them in this dismal place. Two women were clearly fighting cancer for the last time, with no strength left for another round. The words "I give up" were written all over their faces. I'm not saying the room was killing them. I don't know their personal journeys. But I do know that oppressive, dingy, cramped atmosphere didn't help. It felt like whoever had thrown this room together any old way had accepted that "I give up" is the ambience of cancer. And that was just plain wrong.

The only light in that dismal place came from the nurses. One particular nurse, Rosemary, talked tough and handled me rough. One day, while putting in my port, Rosemary poked my increasingly sore throat. "Ow, that hurt!" I said.

She eyeballed me with a straight face. "Honey, no point complaining to me. I don't have a heart, I have a gizzard." I took to calling her Nurse Gizzard, but she was just the opposite.

I saw Nurse Gizzard put her hands on patients and pray. She did not force her faith on people, she just didn't hide it. If they were open to it and needed a lift, she would give that to them, a shared moment of communion with another soul. I felt God's presence when she did that, felt the truth of Matthew 18:20: *For where two or three are gathered together in My name, I am there in the midst of them.*

Nurse Gizzard told me, "This is my church. The souls that

come here are at their most vulnerable, and I've been called here as a nurse to care for them and comfort them. So if they're open to me witnessing or sharing fellowship with them, then that's part of my calling too."

Maybe it was her conviction that influenced what I decided to do, reminded me I had a calling too. Maybe it was seeing how these nurses and their patients were all fighting an uphill battle in a dark place. Whatever the reason, it occurred to me I was not only a patient but also a man of means and a leader who knew plenty about management. Somewhere inside me still lived Mom's little preacher, and I felt God whisper to me that it was time to use that gift for good.

I sent an email to the hospital's CEO, which read, in part:

...I know we don't know each other well, but I will tell you that when I see an opportunity that can change, significantly, those lives that have (in many cases) no hope, faith, belief or a fire to fight like what cancer brings to us that have it and a minimal financial investment and an absolute ROI [return on investment] in less than a year (if not less) – everyone wins. Maybe one of the easiest business decisions we can make in our careers. Our reputations at home, in the community and to all those that we have never met – can be clearly validated in both our professional and personal legacy...

This can't be just paint on the walls and updated furniture and wall hangings. We can't wait until the new building shows up in a couple of years. By the way, I think having a new wing or facility is a great idea. In the meantime, we need to get going. Here are my thoughts based on what I've seen.

1. We need to bump out the back wall to increase additional patients "work stations." This is where currently there is a small waiting area

2. I know the elevators will create a challenge as the back elevators are for service only. To get to the 3rd floor surgical areas, the service elevators might need to become patient elevators. There's got to be another way to get the trash down.

3. We need to update all the easy cosmetics of paint, artwork, furniture, lights and some minimal cabinetry.

4. We need to create a small office area as you walk in the door for "check in." It needs to feel enclosed and more intimate. NOT ALL PATIENTS ARE DEALING WITH THE SAME LEVEL OF DIGNITY during this. We need to really support those that are hurting the most. Privacy is important.

5. There must be at least two "suites" for laying down where one or two patient visitors can sit with chemo patient and have an enclosed space for privacy. THIS IS BIG…I have sat with a couple of women who are in some dark, dark places. Again, it goes back to sensitive effort and dignified privacy in these moments. This would go a long way and would be the most impactful change for everyone…

There is a big opportunity with marketing, local media, social and digital through MH, Panera Bread and many other vehicles…I can be a big voice as a soon to be cancer survivor that went through the MH treatment. Would be happy to get out front. That said, my single biggest mission here is this, I don't want God to put me through a stroke, open heart surgery, a difficult stay in the ICU, diagnosed with throat cancer and then win that battle.....ALL in 10 months with 100% of my time in the Memorial Hermann health care system and not find the biggest and most impactful way I can give back to all those that are facing the same stroke, heart and cancer challenges that I did. To watch the folks being wheeled into the cardiac unit after open heart surgery with no family waiting on them to sitting next to a woman today who is broken and I think, giving up....I can't do it.

...Hope all is well and let me know when you would like to connect.

Keith Isbell
Chief Operating Officer
Rolling Dough, Ltd...
Burger Barons, LLC...

The CEO didn't reply. Over the next few days, I sent emails to several other hospital executives, telling them I was going to make a big donation and start the remodeling process myself. I told them to pass the word on to the CEO. I kept doing this for a few days until the CEO, COO, and another executive all showed up at the infusion room one day without warning. They squeezed the visit between their 8:45 and 11:00 meetings. The trio then walked me from the infusion room to a nearby conference room.

I was pale, losing hair, losing weight. Chemo was deteriorating my body. I had radiation burns on my neck. They looked at me the way people do when they try not to stare, the way people do when they feel not respect but pity.

I didn't let that bother me. After my heart surgery, fear no longer had power over me. Oh, I still *felt* fear, but I walked in faith. In body I felt weak and powerless, but in spirit I felt passionate about helping my fellow patients. I knew I had more credibility on the subject of cancer patients and their needs at this moment than I would once I became cancer free. I doubted I'd have such a perfect opportunity again. Now was the time to speak. Now, before the radiation burns to my throat cost me my voice.

So I spoke, without hesitation. "I've got to ask a question: Have you guys been to the infusion room?"

"Yes," two of them said in unison—the COO, a man, and the third exec, a woman.

"Then you ought to be ashamed."

The CEO, a man, chimed in, "What are you talking about?"

I explained, "Per square foot, you guys are generating money, but in the room where people go to get chemo, a room where people are fighting for their lives, you don't even have the decency to throw up a new coat of paint or encouraging signs or some chairs from this century? At the very least, you could replace the four-dollar sign on the door that says 'Multipurpose Room' with a sign that at least hints you know why we're here."

Since my heart surgery, I had come to believe God put me through every stage of my life for a purpose. I knew I was going to beat cancer. All right then, if cancer was not here to kill me, then why was it here? To me, this meeting was the reason, this opportunity to capture the attention of people with the power to change things, to convince them to take care of my fellow patients in the manner they deserved.

As sick as I felt, I knew I had enough fight in me to overcome whatever obstacles Satan threw in my way, including the depressing Multipurpose Room. But what about the other people in that room who had no fight left? I knew I would be done with treatment in four weeks, but hundreds would sit in those uncomfortable chairs after me.

The first day I had sat next to 65-year-old Johnny, he kept

repeating that all he wanted was a blueberry muffin from the cafeteria, but he didn't have anyone to go down and get one for him. After that, I started bringing him a muffin every day, plus chicken noodle soup and sandwiches for everyone who still had an appetite. Now I was talking to the top mucky-mucks in the hope that my friends could sit in comfortable chairs to eat the snacks I brought, install their chemo ports in a room with a little privacy, maybe be surrounded by bright new paint and encouraging posters during the hours they sat there with poison dripping into their bodies.

Just in case the execs were tempted to blow me off as some emotional patient working out his mortality issues, I made it clear I was a leader like them and an experienced problem solver: "As a restaurant owner, I've remodeled a lot of properties, and I know all these things are easy fixes. This room can be rearranged so patients have a better experience. We can build private chemo rooms so people can have dignity. When you're sick, you don't want to be in a cramped room crowded with a bunch of people."

I also told them what an ordeal it was for someone undergoing the brutal effects of radiation and chemo to have to cross a street, walk past several buildings, and ride an elevator several floors to get to another treatment, no matter what the room was like. "To you it's nothing, but to someone that's sick, it's a marathon to get there. We can do something about this." They listened with real interest, looked me in the eye, gave me firm handshakes. "We'll be in touch with you."

I said, "You need to be in touch with me, because either way I'll be in touch with *you.*"

They laughed, not at me but with me, a laugh that said, we know you mean business, we admire that, and we're excited to be onto something that might actually be important.

The next day I walked into the Multipurpose Room for my chemo, and Nurse Gizzard rushed up to me and threw her arms around me.

"What did you do?" she asked.

"I don't know," I said, confused.

"Yesterday afternoon, we had six executives in this room talking about remodeling and making changes. They mentioned you—by name. By the way, they're already changing the sign on the door from 'Multipurpose Room' to 'Life and Hope Room.' They're doing that today." Then Nurse Gizzard blessed me, right there in the Life and Hope Room.

In the days to come, a new CEO came on board—not because of my letters or anything, the timing was a coincidence—and kept moving forward on many of my suggestions. Meanwhile, the COO and the third exec called and emailed me with regular updates on the hospital's plans to paint the infusion room, put in new chairs, put up inspirational posters, create privacy rooms, and more. One of the third exec's emails read, in part:

Hi Keith,

It was a pleasure meeting you last week...

Your candid feedback is genuinely appreciated and very timely. With its acquisition of the Northeast Hospital from the Northeast Hospital Authority last year, Memorial Hermann has begun to invest in facilities and programs on the campus and in the community. Our needs exceed our capital capacity; but our plans do include investments in the Oncology Service Line; and specifically in the Cancer Center where we need new and larger infusion space. I particularly like the idea of renaming of the infusion suite to "Life and Hope Center." It reflects the energy, strength and courage that cancer patients have while undergoing treatment in that center. Thank you for your interest in working with us. I welcome your involvement and generous offer to contribute towards making this vision a reality...

Best Regards,

————————

I saw this cancer did not have to be a curse but could instead be the beginning of God's new path for me. That did not mean it was an easy path.

In my seventh week, on my last day of radiation, I felt so weak the technicians wanted to send me home in a wheelchair before I even received my treatment. I used my last ounce of strength to croak through my burned-up throat, "I'm not modifying out!" I sat in the waiting room, threw up, fell asleep, and refused to leave... until finally someone came to get me and give me my radiation.

The next day I finished my last radiation and chemo treatments. It's traditional for cancer patients at that hospital to ring a bell after their last treatment. I invited a bunch of people to my bell ringing: my wife, kids, extended family, friends, employees, neighbors. Dozens of supporters gathered around the bell, which hung in a hall just outside the Life and Hope Room. I invited the hospital's CEO and COO too.

Before I rang the bell, I gave a little speech: "I didn't want this. Make no mistake about it. You don't want to hear 'stage four throat cancer,' any more than you want to hear you've got an aneurism sitting on your aortic arch, or that you've just had a stroke... But I'm here, and I'm here for a reason, and I'm here with purpose... I walk these halls with these people and I sit up in that infusion room with people that are fighting for their lives, and in fact many of them have already given up. I don't want any part of this. But if I'm gonna sit here, I've gotta find what I'm supposed to be doing."

I told them that I knew I could look at the devil and say, "get behind me," that I knew I was going to survive, but that those things weren't enough. The question was: what would I do while I was here, what could I do for these patients? "They cry up and down [this hall] and in the infusion room, curl up in balls because their bodies hurt so much. They're fighting for the third or fourth time. It's not too much [for me] to sit down, have a conversation with some very well-respected people here at the hospital...to say, 'Hey, can we do something about it?' So, I wanted to say that for two reasons: number one, to thank you for all the time you've given, and number two, to put a little more pressure on you guys."

Everyone laughed, including the CEO and COO, the kind of laughter that said we were all in this together.

Then I rang the bell so hard I accidentally yanked the pull-chord out. No problem. I just kept that chord in my hands and whipped the bell again. I thought that would wrap up the ceremony, but the radiation doctor asked if she could address the group. She said that usually the doctors and nurses strive to give strength, encouragement, and inspiration to their patients, but that *I* had given those things to *them*. "I think there's a reason our paths crossed here," she told me. "You have really inspired our cancer center and that's going to make it greater. I feel very blessed to have you be my patient, and you are like a gift to us."

Johnny, the older guy who had sat next to me through many a

treatment, who had bitched with me about the horrors of the infusion room, rang the bell the same day as me, and I think he was a little overwhelmed by the crowd I'd gathered. We both knew I didn't have the energy to talk to all of them. Looking back at that video, I looked strong and fit. But I didn't feel it.

Here's what most of the crowd didn't know, that Johnny and I did know: things were about to get worse.

One night a few weeks earlier, my wife, knowing I would soon lose the ability to taste, had made my favorite homemade dish: crawfish with pasta. But she was too late. That was the day my taste buds went. I tried to eat the meal she'd spent more than an hour preparing, but I could not taste it at all, and much as I wanted to spare Annette, I couldn't pretend I did. I was surprised at how unpleasant it felt to force myself to chew something with no flavor, especially considering how much it hurt to swallow it. That meal made me sadder than I expected. It felt like I was losing my ability to enjoy life.

The doctors had warned me that my taste buds would be the first thing to go and that worse was coming. Everyone had warned me—doctors, nurses, and fellow cancer patients—that the worst hell came after the bell rang. I had faith that I could face it. Now I would find out if that was true.

CHAPTER TWENTY-ONE

THE VISITING ANGEL

For He will command His angels concerning you to guard you in all your ways - Psalm 91:11

I knew the next three weeks would be the worst, the three weeks after chemicals had accumulated in my body until it became a toxic swamp. That was the point the doctors sent me home to see if I could survive what they'd done to wreck my body. I thought I was ready to be in the arena, to fight the great fight, but I had not pictured fighting would mean lying flattened in my bed. It felt like I was dying. Because I *was* dying. The chemo and radiation were killing everything in their path, including my healthy cells. There could only be one survivor: cancer or me. But "dying" and "dead" are not the same, and I had faith I could turn this around.

I needed to bring all my strengths to bear on this fight if I was going to tip the balance in my favor: physical strength, mental strength, emotional strength, and spiritual strength. The way I saw it: physical strength meant taking care of my body, emotional strength meant taking my focus off what I couldn't do and switching it to what I could do, mental strength meant visualizing my outcome so I could take the steps to move toward it, and spiritual strength meant keeping my heart in a spirit of gratitude and putting myself in God's hands.

That is, God's hands *and* my family's hands. I recognized this was an important moment in my life for turning inward, not only inward to my personal strengths but also to my strongest relationships. I had decided early on that I didn't want to see anybody once I started feeling the sickest, nobody except my closest family members: Annette, the kids, my dad, and my sister. I saw family as my fifth strength.

There were moments when the idea that I had any strengths at all seemed pathetic. At my sickest point I couldn't get out of bed, so I asked Annette and the kids to come in the room with me to watch a movie. Truth was, I had zero desire to watch a movie. I just wanted to be with them, and a movie was as good an excuse as any. I knew that if I spent too much time alone I might be tempted to think, "This is it, I'm through." The only thing that held that thought at bay on my darkest days was my family. Their strength helped me hold up my faith.

Although I shrank the physical circle around me to family only, I did find a way to involve a larger community of support. Early on, I had watched a YouTube video of a guy who went through cancer treatment, and he explained that community support was important, but that it helped to compartmentalize that support system. He said something to the effect of: "Start your own Facebook group, and put people in that group that you want to keep up to speed with what's going on. That way you keep your cancer life separate from the rest of your life, so cancer doesn't become your identity." I followed his wise advice by starting The Fighter's Corner on FB, for my extended family, friends, neighbors, employees, and colleagues. The more people heard about it, the more people messaged me to include them.

"We're praying for you. We want to be in the loop," they said.

I decided to invite my baseball boys too. I thought about everything I had tried to teach them about teamwork, perseverance, and commitment to excellence, about overcoming obstacles and standing your ground to fight the good fight. Inviting them to witness my journey on The Fighter's Corner gave me the opportunity to put my money where my mouth was, to coach them in a real-life fight. I didn't know if I would survive, but I decided that wasn't the point. So, I made a statement of faith and shared it with them online. A lot of people wouldn't want to involve anybody in that kind of pressure, but I could think of no better way to demonstrate commitment to my life's purpose than to chronicle my path to winning. I expected to win, and I knew that even if I lost I would still win, because God was with me. My cancer journey would be my testimony to them, the ultimate coachable moment.

Every day I felt well enough to post on Facebook, to share my mileposts and thoughts on this journey, I did. Some days I didn't feel well enough to open my laptop or even hold my phone, so Annette would post updates for me. Throughout it all, group members would post their support and encouragement:

- Your tenacity and strength in facing this head on with faith in the One that created you – is remarkable.
- When strength fails, angels hold you.
- Thanks Coach for the great life lessons both on and off the field.
- Keep on fighting, you got this.
- In life we struggle at times. But He who lives in us is greater. Keith, this is the beginning of the victory before you.

The group support helped give me strength when I felt weak,

but more than that, I felt as if together we were sharing a story of God's grace that would continue long after my cancer journey ended. If anyone in that group ever goes through a life-or-death struggle, or any kind of struggle, they can always go back to The Fighter's Corner and re-read the thread from start to finish to re-mind themselves of my journey, and motivate them to have faith in their own journeys.

All that is not to say there weren't moments when I felt alone. As predicted, things got hardest during the three weeks after I rang the bell. I spent most of those three weeks unable to rise from my bed. I had blisters inside and out: blisters on my neck, thirty sores inside my mouth and those were just the ones I could see and count, and I could only imagine what the inside of my throat looked like. I felt like a hunk of meat burned alive, which I suppose I was, come to think of it. My taste buds were gone, and my saliva was quick to follow. Swallowing was impossible, so my oncologist installed a feeding tube. I went without solid food for three and a half months. The feeding tube helped keep critical nutrients in my body to prevent starvation, but it was not the healthiest way to eat. By Easter weekend, I was down sixty pounds, and it was not as if I were fat to begin with. No doubt I lost muscle along the way.

If I went to the bathroom to throw up, even with the door shut, my daughter, Sophie, would cry hysterically. The vomiting alone sounded horrific enough because my throat was raw from radia-tion. But I insisted on making even louder noises than necessary, until it sounded like I was throwing up internal organs. Here's why I did that: I found that if I made dramatic retching noises, nothing would come up. This seemed like a positive result to me because I didn't want to lose any more weight. I was only getting a thou-sand calories a day in my feeding tube, and I knew if I threw it up that would mean too many calories-out compared to calories-in. I felt determined to hold it in, even to the point of swallowing my own puke. To me, that retching noise was the sound of me fighting back, but to Sophie, it must have sounded like an alarm signaling that my death was imminent.

Sophie never said, "Oh Dad, please don't do that." But she would get up, go into her room, shut the door, and sob. Her sobs were not as loud as my vomiting, but we could all hear her. She was 15 and terrified I would die. My mom died when I was 15. I couldn't bear the thought of putting Sophie through that, to the point that I couldn't bear the thought of her even considering the possibility of my death. She had already been traumatized by sitting in the car with me when I had my stroke, so in her mind my survival must have seemed unlikely. Too much had happened.

I took to running into the backyard when I felt nauseous so my daughter wouldn't hear me puke, but also in case she did, so I didn't have to hear her sobs. I knew both of us were trying to spare each other, but we didn't have much success. And the sound of a grown man in his backyard making sounds like a cat coughing up hairballs must have had the neighbors scratching their heads.

The doctor had prescribed pain patches for me because I didn't deal with pain meds well. But even the patches made me feel so weird, I tried to avoid them. Between the pain, the inability to eat, the nausea, the weight loss, and Sophie's crying, I felt depression and darkness crowding in.

***

Although I lay in bed with my eyes closed or half-closed twenty hours a day, I didn't exactly sleep. I was neither awake nor asleep, but in this floaty twilight between the two where I couldn't think straight. I couldn't tell the difference between my dreams and reality.

One time I half-woke from my half-sleep and declared, "I was with Jesus." I was keeping pen and paper by the bed in anticipation of just those sorts of floating thoughts, which swam around my head through all my sleepless weeks. So, I wrote down, "I was with Jesus." I don't remember writing those words, but Annette heard what I said and saved the paper to show me later. That's the only reason I know it happened.

The only dreams I remember clearly from this time were the ones in which I saw my mother. These were not random childhood memories, not hallucinations of her speaking to me, not dreams full of surreal moments like my usual dreams. These dreams were nothing more or less than the calm and silent reassurance that my mother was with me. These dreams came to me twice. I opened my eyes and told Annette, "I was with my mom."

Annette never questioned it. She accepted it as an unexplained blessing, and so did I.

Throughout my war with cancer, from beginning to end, I felt I was fighting not only for myself but also for my mother, who had lost her own battle with that demon. But even though I saw myself as fighting for her, at that moment I realized she was the one fighting for me, because it was at my darkest moment that I felt her presence, right there, in the room with me. I felt God had sent her because He knew she was the only one who would understand how to comfort me. I'm not saying I saw a ghost. My mother's presence was real and whole to me, even though I could not see her. To this day, I know without a doubt my mother was there, as surely as I knew it was her when she walked into my room to check on me whenever I was sick as a boy.

Once my mom showed up in those final weeks—the worst weeks of all—she never went away. Her presence fell into the background during the moments when the pain was almost tolerable, moments when I lay awake on the couch or bed, surrounded by my wife and kids, watching TV or listening to them talk. But the moments when I felt sickness and death overcoming me, felt alone and abandoned, suffered the kind of pain that seemed infinite, I had only to think "Mom" and my very thoughts brought her presence into the room. Not someone I could touch, but someone whose protective, nurturing arms I could sense around me almost as a physical sensation, not the flesh of her arms themselves, but their warmth, gentle weight, and soothing caress. My mother was always a demonstrative person, who showed affection by physically holding people, always the last one to let go of a hug. I felt covered by her, the way some people feel covered in the Holy Spirit.

Mom always had a brightness to her, and in my darkest days she lit the way to the other side. People always said she was an angel. Maybe she was. I wouldn't be surprised. All I know is this: In life, she used to walk into a room and light it up, and now, as I floated through the shadowy room between life and death she was with me, a candle lighting my way.

I was 48 when I got cancer. My mother was 43 when she died of cancer. My brother was 48 when he was murdered. I felt so many connections between my life and theirs. In the dark, God showed me the connections, and for the first time they didn't seem like a curse, or coincidence, but like a reminder from God that we're all connected, all part of His greater plan.

*****

One night around week three, I stood huddled over in the back-yard, choking and retching but unable to stop myself from puking into one of Annette's flowerbeds. I feared that my extreme faith in the face of these odds was foolish after all, feared that death was winning. For the first time, I felt so alone even God seemed to have abandoned me. I shouted, "God, where are you?"

In my head, I heard God reply with a simple question, "Are you ready to climb out?"

"There you are," my internal voice answered back. Then I said aloud, "Yes!" With that, I walked into the house, straight up to Annette, and even though I had taken to writing most things down, I didn't write this, but croaked it: "This feeding tube's coming out of me. We're never going to use it again."

"Well, we'll talk to the doctors," she said.

"No, I'm done."

And I heard God's voice echo, "Give it to me, I'll handle it."

From that moment on, I knew, whatever I had left in me to push through to victory, I would give to God. The rest, I would rely on Him to do for me. I knew the only thing that would save me in the end was to believe in what Christ promised, that by His stripes I was already healed. I knew if I didn't give myself over to reliance on God, darkness would encompass me. I refused to let that happen.

Here's what happened after I cried out to God in our garden: once I took that feeding tube out, I started to get better. Food tasted like nothing, but I chewed it anyway. It hurt to swallow, but I swallowed anyway, one bite at a time. I began to gain weight. I began to gain strength. I began to feel whole again.

Cancer treatment broke my body down. God broke me down to show me who I was. Now it was time to rebuild myself bite by bite, bit by bit.

I was supposed to have a PET scan to test for any remaining cancer cells six months post-treatment, in September of 2017. Instead, I demanded the doctor order the scan in June, three months early. June was six months from my diagnosis, and I wasn't about to forget what I had declared the day I was diagnosed: "...come June, I'm going to be cancer free."

We had to wait a day for the PET scan results. The longest day.

Then the doctor called. "Keith, it's unbelievable. It's almost like it melted away."

"What does that mean?"

"You're 100% cancer free."

"I told you!"

"I knew you were going to say that."

I hugged Annette, hard, but my joy was too big for our house to contain, so I stepped out the front door and threw both arms in the air in victory before I walked back in and kissed her. Both of us were hugging, jumping up and down, and crying. We repeated this scene with the kids when they came home from their summer activities.

The days that followed overwhelmed me with a "now what?" feeling. Through God's grace, I had dodged death twice. If the first time was a wake-up call, the second felt like a calling. What was God calling me to do? I prayed a lot, and the first answer was that I was called to be healed. Although the cancer was gone, I knew I would need months to fight my way back. Once I bounced back, I knew I would never be the same.

Neither would my family. I wasn't the only one who suffered and needed to heal. Cancer does not just affect the person who has it. My whole family went through cancer.

Through all of it, Annette took care of me in a way that went beyond "for better or worse." She was patient, practical, and persistent in doing whatever had to be done with the kind of devotion that made me understand what a God-centric marriage is all about: she did not act like it was her duty to me, but rather a blessing to her to be allowed to share so many tangible signs of her love. I could never ever pay her back for that. I know Annette lives with a recurring fear that my cancer might come back, or another stroke, or a new heart issue. Yet this knowledge also makes us so much more precious to each other.

Everyone responds to trauma differently, and Sophie seemed to take my confrontation with mortality the hardest, maybe because she was at the most impressionable age among us. Sophie became the family worrier, almost more motherly than her mother, carrying the emotional baggage of my illness. There were times Annette and I feared we were losing our girl down a well of depression, anxiety, and fear. She quit volleyball and extracurriculars because she wanted to be home with me every moment, not just to help but to spend with me what she feared might be my last days.

My son had a more positive response—at least on the surface—to the helplessness of seeing me through three near-death experiences: stroke, heart surgery, cancer. Zach became my at-home doctor. He fed me my nutrient packs through my feeding tube when I was too weak and fumbling to manage it. He slept on the couch, so if I woke up in the delusional looney-land that came with my inability to sleep, he could hear me shuffling in the living room or kitchen, come catch me, and guide me back to bed.

As Zach walked me through our house, I could already see him as a man, and the picture was clear even in my blurry state: there was no doubt he was going to be a doctor. I had known this would mean a lot of work, but hadn't known the first thing about the kinds of scores and grades he would need to achieve even while he was still in high school. Zach knew, though, and at 16 he was on it! He moved from 135th in his class to 31st in a year and a half. His SAT score was 1490. We stopped looking at his homework. We barely looked at his grades anymore. One hundred ten percent of what he did, he did on his own. He had already been to two medical conferences. My heart surgeon showed him around the hospital, not once but twice. The doctor was so impressed with him he got him special permission to sit in on two open-heart surgeries.

Zach decided to apply to the University of Texas, which would require being in the top seven percent of his class. So, he was not only helping to take care of me at home but also working his butt off at his high school's medical-track program. He planned to take four AP courses his senior year. "Man, what is wrong with you?" I teased him.

It was astonishing to see that my son enjoyed studying like it was better than a night on the town. I had passed my father's work ethic down to him like a legacy, but it blew my mind to witness what he had done with it. Zach had decided to become a doctor because a doctor had saved my life, and I realized that he was going to give that to others, was going to give people back their fathers, mothers, sisters, brothers, was going to give what he had been given and what I had been given: a second chance.

And now I was being given a third chance, so I could see him do it. I felt humbled to walk next to him and see that future.

***

I've returned to the hospital several times, to visit with the administrators who have invited me to watch the transformations I instigated in the infusion room, to say hello to the doctors and nurses who saved my life, and to encourage fellow patients who've returned for more treatment. On one of my visits, Johnny was back, the guy who rang the bell the same day I did. This would be his final fight. He only made it another week or so.

Why did I make it when Johnny didn't? I know it's not because I deserve it. The gift of survival came to me through no merit of my own. I didn't want any part of this. My response was not to question, or to take credit by assuming God loves me better, but rather to be grateful and not take this gift for granted. I've made it my mission to give something back.

I'm a living testament to grace, which seems so random. I believed Johnny went on to walk with the Lord, which was its own sort of blessing. Still, I wondered, why was I given more time? What would I do with it?

To this day, I still begin every day with my morning devotional. For half an hour or so, I watch a video by one of several preachers whose spiritual teachings speak to me, study my Bible, meditate, and always finish in prayer. The prayer to me is the most critical part. During that prayer, I lay all my troubles at God's feet. I know I cannot overcome life's obstacles by myself: fear, depression, worry, doubt. When those feelings come knocking at the door, prayer is the only way I know to climb out.

Getting up-close and personal with mortality forced me to see God not only as some perfect entity to believe in but as a caring parent to lean on. Not just a father, a dad.

I didn't think I needed God, thought I could will my way through anything. Then I looked in the rearview mirror at my life up to this point, and saw He had always been there, especially when I'd deserved Him least. I've still never seen scientific evidence that my God is real. I only know my experience. I don't know where my promised land is yet, but I'm headed that direction. Hurdle after hurdle gets put in front of me and I clear it. Then I clear the next one, and the next. Then I run some more, run to win, like my mother taught me.

CHAPTER TWENTY-TWO

THE BIGGER STORM

Have I not commanded you? Be strong and of good courage; do not be afraid, nor be dismayed, for the Lord your God is with you wherever you go. – Joshua 1:9

I don't like to think about Hurricane Harvey. Even witnessing it firsthand, seeing a storm so massive do so much destruction and devastate so many people, I found it hard to fathom.

In some ways, hurricanes are all about speed, about wind and water run amok, but Harvey had to be felt to be believed, with rain so intense each drop hurt when it hit my body. In other ways, hurricanes make time move slowly. For a week, Harvey huddled over Houston and pounded. I watched the waters rise throughout the county and thought a lot about Noah's Ark. Every conceivable body of water—rivers, lakes, ponds, creeks, pools, gutters—all broke their banks, overflowed, and spilled. The water went everywhere. In the first days, nobody was out saving anybody else, except people who had boats. Not because people didn't care, but because it was all anyone could do to keep their own heads above water and get through it.

Harvey was on another level from Ike or any storm I ever imagined. Although I was in the midst of it, I only experienced it from where I sat, so I didn't know much more about what was happening than most Americans with Internet and TV. But the fact that I was watching on a screen the desperation of people who lived in places I knew by heart, made it all feel personal.

I decided to drive over to our Panera in Atascocita, Texas, before the water closed in and the restaurant had to close up. By 1:00 a.m., the news was bad. The storm was staying put. This was going to be ugly. "I want everybody out!" I hollered. "Get your checklist done, put the food in the fridge, get out, and go home."

A day later, I went back to check that restaurant, looked around at our bakery full of food, and thought, *No way am I going to throw this out. There must be people in this community who can use something to eat.* So I logged on to Facebook and posted:

Hey I'm at the Panera in Atascocita. Anyone in need of bakery products, I'll be here another couple of hours. It's all free. You can just take it.

Within minutes, people mobbed the restaurant. Many of them had relocated from mandatory evacuation areas to stay nearby with family and friends, even though Atascocita was only marginally better off than the nearby towns they came from. Households of four had turned into households of twelve overnight. Local grocery stores were closed, and it was hard to get around to find food elsewhere because streets were flooded. People who wondered how they were going to feed their overflowing homes made a line out our front door and down the sidewalk.

"Oh, my goodness, this is bad," I muttered to myself. My hands shook as I passed out food, the only person behind the counter, barely able to keep up with demand, or to comprehend where all these people came from, or what would happen to them when the danishes and bagels ran out.

I knew full well some of these folks weren't going back home after the storm ended, knew some would have no home to return to. I saw on their faces that they knew it too, and it was hitting them in a way that gave them a look beyond sadness. At first, as they stood in line, I saw a darkness hanging over them like a reckoning. But standing there for a couple of hours and handing out food, I saw that we had all become a small light to each other in the dark. I saw in their tentative smiles that, although their individual worlds were collapsing, the sight of a guy passing out loaves of bread when they most needed it gave them hope.

There was something about the restaurant that day that felt like church: people were congregating in a safe haven, sharing fellowship, crying, listening, and finding small blessings to laugh about. I gave them cups to fill with soda from the fountain and invited them to sit at the tables, where they just talked. Most of them were perfect strangers, but it felt like a family reunion in the midst of crisis.

I'll bet I gave food to some 250 people. They cleaned out our bakery in two hours, although a few lingered a little longer, to remind each other they weren't alone.

After that, I got hold of all the managers I could, and found a half-dozen who could still make it around the worst of the flood to reach their restaurants. I told them, "Go in tomorrow and give away everything in the bakery until you're out of it." We used social media to get the word out. Altogether, we probably gave food to more than a thousand people.

This was not me trying to figure out how to be a great guy. This was beyond being the hero or the goat. I just saw the right thing to do and did it. To me doing the right thing meant one simple thing: pay attention and be willing. I wasn't alone, and I did a lot less than many I knew. The guys at my church never slept. They took in hundreds of people for days, giving them not only food, but also shelter and comfort. To me, the real heroes were the pastors and church leaders whose compassion never let up for weeks of unending need.

Annette and I volunteered at the church shelters too. God's second commandment is to love thy neighbor as thyself, and the more evidence I've seen of how stormy life is for every one of us, the more I take that to heart. I feel an obligation to do whatever I can to do my part without reservation or the need to take credit.

As for how Hurricane Harvey affected me: My family lives on a low rise, too low to call a hill but just high enough so our home was spared. Hundreds of homes in our neighborhood stood in six or seven feet of water. Some of our neighbors still had no homes more than a year later.

Hurricane Harvey was a tragedy for Houston, Humble, Conroe, the whole metro area. It was a tragedy for my community, my neighbors, my hometown. My deepest compassion went out to everyone I handed a sandwich or a kind word. Nobody should ever have to go through that. On a personal level, though, Harvey was nothing more or less than a symbol of the bigger storm that 2017 had already put me through. I spent fourteen months weathering that storm, and the only way I found to overcome it was to *be* the storm.

I know I'm not alone in the realization that all of life is a series of storms: tempests that can take a life, a loved one, a home—all in a blink. There's not a one of us that devastation and tragedy fail to visit. What do you do with that? There's nothing to do but deal with it. I've discovered the hard way what can happen if I decide I'm a victim of circumstance. I did that in my youth, after my mom died, and it paralyzed me for years.

Today, I choose not to be defeated by life's storms, but to be motivated by them. Every time I turn around, Satan throws something at me. That's just what he does. But in partnership with God, I win, every time, even when it doesn't look like it.

***

Death took my mother and brother and tried to take me three times, and I can't claim I came away from those experiences a stronger man than before. Instead, I discovered how much strength the Lord had given me all along, and how much of His own strength He wanted me to rely on Him for. The losses and near losses of my life have taught me that I might have limits but there is no limit to hope, that when I have hope it makes my limits of no consequence. Faith is a partnership. I have only to do my job and let God do His. The results have not always looked the way I wanted, but that's not the point. The point is I am now a partner in whatever results God sees fit to give me, and I've learned to see the gift in that.

I was once convinced God did not exist. Now I'm closer to God than I was back when I was Mom's little preacher. Back when I was doing drugs and drinking like a madman, I was an atheist. After I made myself into a restaurant manager, got married, and had kids, I became a lukewarm, in-name-only Christian. I probably figured I could talk my way into heaven if it came down to it. After all, I never did anything so bad it seemed unforgivable. The problem was, whatever I did or said, it was all about me.

If I could sit down with the younger version of me, this is what

I'd tell him: "Don't fear. Don't ever give up on anything. Know that pain is temporary but God is real, and He never leaves your side, not even when you don't believe in Him. Most of all: love yourself. Every day you don't is a day wasted. Don't buy into the lie that you aren't good enough. Because you are." I've learned that loving myself does not spring from ego, but from gratitude for being the man God made me, for the purpose He has given me. Loving myself requires me to recognize that gift so I can put it to good use. If I love God, I have to love all His creation, and that includes me.

I've found the warrior in me, and since then I've come to see that a warrior lives in each person I encounter, though not everyone discovers it. Sometimes it takes hard knocks to learn our strengths and how to use them. It's up to us whether we rise to the occasion, and then whether we keep putting our strength into practice in our daily lives.

Everyone's talents and abilities are unique, but as I look around me, I see evidence that we all have four types of strength: mental toughness, spiritual toughness, physical toughness, and emotional toughness.

For me, mental toughness is the will to do whatever it takes to overcome life's obstacles, motivating myself to deal with dark days by envisioning myself on the other side of them. Spiritual toughness is the belief I am complete because God made me that way, and the faith to lean on Him for whatever strengths I lack. Physical toughness means getting up on the days I don't think I can, being active, and not retreating when I feel beaten but instead rising to my feet and getting back into the world. Emotional toughness means speaking my truth and responding to challenges with a positive approach. I'm not talking about pretending life isn't tough, putting on phony cheerfulness, or refusing to admit defeat. I'm talking about pushing through all of the emotional ups and downs of life with the trust that, whatever I feel now, good or bad, God loves me, and that with Him I can get through anything.

My spirit of gratitude is bottomless because I insist on it, especially when the voice of doubt shows up. Sometimes I don't feel grateful at all but resentful, and that's when it's most important to express gratitude. When I do, the resentment recedes. This is a gift from God, who doesn't just ask us, "in everything give thanks," but who also fills us with the very thankfulness He requires. He doesn't do this for Himself, but for us, for me, because He knows I need it, because He knows the gift of gratitude is the key to a full life.

I lived most of my life in fear of cancer, even when I didn't have it. That fear did not help me one bit: didn't prevent it, didn't cure it, didn't arm me to fight it. There's healthy fear and unhealthy fear, and I've come to learn the difference. I believe worry, anxiety, and stress are the primary reasons for all doctor's visits in the U.S. For all I know, my fear contributed to my cancer. I'm not blaming myself, or anyone with cancer. Nobody deserves that evil disease. I'm just saying I'm not giving cancer one more inch of ground to stand on if I can help it. The rest I leave to God. I know I cannot control everything, but fretting over that doesn't change it.

One hundred percent of us will die at some point, but getting close to death has given me a better perspective on what it means to live. I no longer live in fear, I just live in reality, which is the other side of fear. When fear and doubt come knocking these days, I meet them at the door and say, God knows all about you, and your services are not needed today. Sometimes they go on their way, sometimes they come in and sit a while, but they never take over, not anymore. I live fearlessly, and ever since I decided to do that, I live without regret.

There's a tremendous amount of freedom in seeing life in terms of its ending. The need to be in control is a joke. Chasing money is a joke. Yes, I want to be paid for the value I provide, but I'll no longer sacrifice my soul to give in to illusions of security, or sacrifice my relationship with the people I love to achieve illusions of success. What a waste. My perspective has changed for one reason: I went toe-to-toe with death. If that doesn't change a person, then that person has issues.

After all my family and I had been through, probably nobody would have blamed me if I'd considered my cancer diagnosis a death sentence and given up. Instead I chose to have faith that I would win. Certainly, I knew we were going to walk through The Valley of the Shadow of Death. During those dark days, my wife cried and my kids walked around in a cloud of uncertainty. Just because I declared unwavering faith at the outset, did not mean I avoided moments of doubt. Many of them. Yet at those doubtful moments, I leaned on God, and God heard me.

As I stood outside throwing up on Easter weekend, I made up my mind I was done with doubt and fear. I knew then, even as I could barely stand on two wobbly legs, I was already running toward a new purpose. I got rid of my feeding tube, tore off my pain patch, and climbed out of the dark. I'm now cancer free and fulfilling my new purpose.

I don't have to work at it anymore, at those things that give my life meaning: family, faith, and legacy. Especially family. I used to have to force my schedule into a shape that let me squeeze time in with my son. Now I simply want to talk to my son and daughter, to ask about their day, spend time with them. If something else falls by the wayside because of that, so be it.

Nothing to do with family feels like work anymore. I used to show up to Christmas and Thanksgiving celebrations, but rarely picked up the phone to talk to my father, siblings, aunts, uncles, nieces, nephews, and cousins. I used to miss funerals and weddings if they got in the way of work. Now I miss work sometimes when it gets in the way of family.

Chapter Twenty-three

A Humbler Man

This is the unwanted chapter, the chapter I never planned to write. June 12 of this year was my one-year anniversary of finding out I was cancer free. It was also time for my PET scan to see if I could still make that claim. I got the scan, then a couple of days later I got the call from my oncologist. "I got the report, Keith, but I think it's best you come in so we can look at it together." I knew this wasn't good, otherwise she would have said, Yay, everything's perfect, just move on with your life. This time I sat alone in her office while she pointed out two spots that lit up on the scan.

"So, how long do I have to live?" I asked.

She didn't dance around. "In most cases, with a recurrence of cancer, we say about a year—"

That knocked the wind out of me. "One year? That doesn't work for me. I've got a lot of life to live."

"Wait," she said, "I wasn't finished. With where you're at, the way you live, the attitude you have, you're probably more in the three- to five-year mark. The ones who beat this back down tend to be the determined ones, the fighters like you."

At that moment, I didn't feel like a fighter. I felt defeated. Suddenly I had a shelf life. Everything was about to change again.

An abyss opened at my feet and it was hard to feel anything but dizzy considering it.

I went home to an empty house. Annette was out of town. I called and gave her the news. She grew emotional, but I can't say she didn't take it well, because I've learned there's no good way to take bad news. Then I called my dad and my older sister Leslie. We all cried, and as bad as it felt, I was grateful that we could shed those tears together, that we were still a family. Hardest of all was sitting down with the kids when Annette got home. They were sad, but this time was different. This time, we were a family that had faced death more than once and we were still thriving. Whatever happened, we were together, and we knew—we *know*—that's what matters most.

I had a serious talk with my business partner about moving forward with this new uncertainty. Mark was empathetic, but it didn't feel like we were preparing to say goodbye to our partnership or anything like that. We've had plenty of challenges with our business, and we simply saw this as the next one. We discussed one-year, three-year, and five-year scenarios, and remained open to the possibility of more. I wanted to focus on that last possibility: on more, on overcoming, on miracles. But if I started from that point, it would not feel fair to the people around me. I did not know God's plan, only that everyone's time on earth is limited, and doctors were suggesting for the first time that my limit might come sooner than I planned.

I have two high school kids bound for college. My son has been accepted into the University of Texas, a blessing in the midst of turmoil. As a 49-year-old father, husband, and business owner, with so many people counting on me, it seems important to be both hopeful *and* pragmatic. The greatest of faith promises eternal life in heaven but not immortality on this earth.

That's not to say I'm giving up. Not even a little. I'm pressing forward the way people do who understand that none of us know how long we have. I haven't stopped sharing my testimony at speaking engagements. However, the conversation is shifting. I've given more talks than I can count on the themes of hope and encouragement: I beat heart disease, I beat cancer. These days I have to finish with, "Oh, by the way..."

How do I accept my mortality and still demonstrate a passion for living? That's the question God has handed me. It's easier to tell a story when it ends with certainty, up or down. It's harder to finish a story when so much is unknown. But that's the way God tells stories. Life's greatest lessons are not always about victories. In moments of victory, it's tempting to drift from our relationship with God because those are moments that appeal to ego. I'm always drawn closer to God in the middle of struggle.

I'll admit, sometimes in my silent prayers, I tell Him, "I get it. I've felt Your grace in the dark. I've seen the light. I get what matters. How much more do I need to go through for You to know You have my full attention? I'm with You, God. Can we ease up on the struggle for a while? At the very least, can You show me whatever You want to show me and spare my family from going through this again?" But I try not to get caught in the "Why me?" moments for long, because it's a fast slide from that to letting myself play the victim. That I won't do.

I believe a miracle is coming. Why wouldn't I after everything I've experienced? I am where I am in life thanks to miracle after miracle. I know God isn't finished with me on this earth. Not yet. He's still trimming me down to the man I need to be to give Him the glory. Whatever miracle God gives, whether it's to heal me, heal someone else, or do something else entirely, I know it will be something that will give people hope in the face of challenges. That message has repeated itself in my life so often. God and I are on the same page there.

I don't get to be a lukewarm Christian after this diagnosis. No matter what, God is my healer. Whether He heals my cancer or not, He always heals *me*. If this mountain won't be moved, if I draw my last breath, that changes nothing in the grand scheme. Am I going to say, "Then I guess God wasn't real"? No way. I've picked a side, and I'm all in.

***

Panera Corporate knows about my diagnosis, and being the fans they are of my work and my leadership, they sent my franchise operation a bunch of bracelets printed with the words: Team Isbell. My leadership team was at a meeting where they received these bracelets to wear and to pass out to their employees, and it got back to me that one of my directors griped, "I wish I didn't have to wear this bracelet. I wish I could turn this around so I didn't have to see this name. I guess I have to wear this until he goes into remission or dies?"

When word got back to me, I wanted to sit him down and ask, "Man, what's wrong with you?" We go back a long way. I hired him when he was a senior in high school, and I've promoted him right up the chain for fifteen years. I'll admit, I felt a little betrayed. Upon reflection now, I realize people can act pretty dysfunctional when confronted with the specter of cancer. I hope he only said that because he was worried for me, because he doesn't want to think about bad things happening to me, because he was already grieving my loss and wanted to get it over with. I wish I could make him understand, I'm still here, man! Don't write me off yet, because I'm sure not.

Having cancer means spending a lot of time at hospitals, surrounded by thousands of people who are sick, and hundreds who are dying. I see how some of them wear their disease like an identity, while others look sick too but carry themselves differently, as if to say, this illness is something I have but it's not who I am. I believe that attitude increases their chances of winning tremendously. When I'm tempted to speak the word "cancer," I replace it with the word "hope" every chance I get.

I don't think I'm the next Job. I don't believe God is sitting in heaven saying, let me throw all I have at this guy and see if he can take it. I don't think God curses people with disease. I think there is a natural flow to life. I also believe there is free will. But I have faith that God intervenes from time to time, and that His timing has a purpose. If this had happened to me twenty-five years ago, I would have played the victim because I was closed off to the idea of anything greater than myself. Even a dozen years ago, I was a lukewarm Christian, a John 3:16 Christian, who believed "For God so loved the world, that he gave his only begotten Son, that whosoever believeth in him should not perish, but have everlasting life." Which is true and beautiful, but not the whole story.

The whole story calls us to work. God calls me to work. I don't get to sit and stare at the sky and say, "Where's my miracle? I'm ready!" I don't expect to pray and receive divine healing without doing my part. I take care of myself, eat right, exercise, and go to my treatments. More important, I make time for family and friends, and I make time for my spiritual growth.

Not all the work feels very spiritual. Treatment can be a downright drag. I started with immunotherapy, but the cancer continued to progress. So, I moved to a new course of chemotherapy, which was no fun the first time around. I'm never doing radiation again. That was the worst. I know who I am, how I am, what I can take. I'm adding alternative medications to my treatment. I'm opening myself to a wider world. I'm discovering God is all around me, in every choice I make, every place I go, every person I touch, everyone who touches me.

My family is doing better this time around. Annette and I are coming to terms with mortality. We're always honest with the kids about what's going on. I've never forgotten the unexpected shock of losing my mom, so I've promised myself I'll always be straight with my kids even if it's hard. Zach responds with greater strength, more determined than ever to become a doctor. Sophie responds with unanswerable questions, like: "Is Dad going to be okay?" They each deal in their own way. The best their mom and I can do for them is hold onto each other as we walk through this, keeping faith in the face of uncertainty.

How do we answer Sophie's questions? We tell her what the doctors say, then we tell her what the Bible says, "By His stripes we are healed." My mother kept that quote posted next to her deathbed. To her last she never wavered in showing us her absolute belief in miracles.

Someday I'll take my last breath. The day I do, I'll know where my heart is, I'll know where my soul is. Between now and then, I remain God's humble servant.

I've always felt the need to be the strongest guy in the room, to take care of everyone, to never show weakness. But these days I'm sometimes humbled by doubt. Little by little, I'm learning to let go of doubt and hang on to the humility. God is showing me its gifts.

I recently attended the dedication ceremony for the new Life and Hope Suites at the hospital, which replaced the infusion room and much of the old cancer wing. Everything has moved to the other side of the campus, and this is a miracle in its own right. There are now private rooms for those who need them, no more community rooms where people in various stages of cancer are forced to stare at each other if they're not up for it—not all of us are fighting the same fight. I was thrilled that they listened to my ideas about things like the need for windows. I remember feeling claustrophobic, surrounded by the dim walls of the old multipurpose room. Now, looking out the windows, patients can see blue sky and distant horizons, can see the sun come out after a storm, can see the possibility of life beyond these walls.

The Life and Hope Wing helps cancer patients with an outlook of dignity and hope. I only had to get cancer to help set that project rolling. I hope He plans to use me to help Him work more miracles—not me, but God working through me. I now know the humility required.

***

I've wrestled with the Angel of Death on so many levels, but those fights have given me the gift of a story. It's a story of encouragement, inspiration, and support for others as they suit up for their own battles. When God gives you a story, you tell it. That has become my life's purpose.

I wish I could give everybody around me a pill to see life the way I do now, to see the world the way I do, to see people the way I do—even strangers. I don't know where we're all headed or where I'm headed, but I know if I do whatever I do in a spirit of thanksgiving, the direction will take care of itself.

In April of 2017, when I was wrestling cancer maybe as hard as Jacob wrestled God's own angel, I mentally planned my own funeral. Since then I've been living with my eulogy in mind, the eulogy in which family, faith, and legacy drive my every choice. At my eulogy, whenever that day comes, I hope someone will be able to honestly express something like this: "Keith was a family man, to his wife, his children, his friends, his employees, his neighbors, to humanity. In everything Keith did, he gave God the glory, he was a good example to his kids in how to live, and he made a difference in the life of everyone he met, even if just in the way he shook the hands of a stranger and let that stranger know he mattered." And here it is now, in black and white, just in case anyone feels like quoting me.

I want my redemption to be a gift to others. When someone says, "I can't take it anymore," I want to tell them what I've been through. I want to give them hope, and I notice that as long as I give God the glory, He sees fit to keep my schedule busy with opportunities to do just that. So many people want to hear my story. I've shared it with organizations that support cancer patients and cancer research, with the American Heart Association, with audiences ranging from a dozen to a thousand. Coaches for several youth sports teams have asked me to give their kids motivational talks, including my daughter's volleyball coach.

I recently talked to a youth group, and one of the kids was a teenage girl whose parents abandoned her when she was small. She wrote me a note that said my story gave her hope. She was not talking about the hope of overcoming illness or death, but the hope that even someone whose family has been torn apart can find their way back to family, can find their way home.

Panera Corporate found out about what my team and I did during Hurricane Harvey and invited me to share our story with company execs and franchise owners. I gave a talk at their national meeting in the fall of 2017, and I did tell them a little bit about what we did during Harvey. But in the end, I spent most of my time at the podium talking about all of life's storms. I talked about my heart, my cancer, my mother, my brother, all the moments life takes us to our knees: "How do you handle that? You just look in front of you to see what needs to be done, and you do it. The way we dealt with Harvey was no different." I reminded them that they never know who's working next to them, who's living next door, who's sitting next to them in church. All around us, people are walking through storms we can't see, and as people in the business of serving others, we have an opportunity to reach out a hand and show them someone cares.

I finished with Joshua 1:9. "'Have I not commanded you? Be strong and of good courage; do not be afraid, nor be dismayed, for the Lord your God *is* with you wherever you go.'" Those multimillionaires rose to their feet in a standing ovation.

God gave me the gift of gab, so I'm using it in hopes it will serve as an umbrella, a wall of sandbags, a rescue helicopter, or whatever folks might find useful to help them weather their storms. I'm still Mom's little preacher, preaching on the Walls of Jericho. And the walls keep tumbling down. It's a good life, for as long as I can live it. Thank God for that.

I don't know what's going to happen to me. But then, none of us does. If I die tomorrow or fifty years from now, it will be without regret. What a run it has been. I'm not just running to win now, Mom, I'm running to live.

Made in the USA
Lexington, KY
30 November 2018